PAPPAS & MORIN, PH.D

TRUMP
DERANGEMENT
SYNDROME

A psychological analysis
of leftist ideology

ISBN-13: 978-1-963102-24-6 (Paperback)
ISBN-13: 978-1-963102-23-9 (eBook)
ISBN-13: 978-1-963102-25-3 (Hardcover))

Published by Defiance Press and Publishing, LLC

Bulk orders of this book may be obtained by contacting Defiance Press and Publishing, LLC. www.defiancepress.com.

Public Relations Dept. – Defiance Press & Publishing, LLC
281-581-9300
pr@defiancepress.com

Defiance Press & Publishing, LLC
281-581-9300

info@defiancepress.com

*To all of those who have committed to
defend our freedom and democracy.*

CONTENTS

You have no enemies, you say?
Alas! my friend, the boast is poor;
He who has mingled in the fray
Of duty, that the brave endure,
Must have made foes! If you have none,
Small is the work that you have done.
You've hit no traitor on the hip,
You've dashed no cup from perjured lip,
You've never turned the wrong to right,
You've been a coward in the fight.

- Charles Mackay Scottish Author, Poet
1814-1889

Trump Derangement Syndrome ...

Many believe it all started June 16, 2015 with the infamous ride down the escalator in Trump Tower. However, from my personal observation, Trump Derangement Syndrome (TDS) was in its infancy many years earlier. Donald Trump has always been a polarizing individual, although certainly not to the degree he has become in this post millennium period. In this book, I will attempt to peel back the layers and expose how and why Donald Trump has evolved to become one of the most talked about American presidents in history, and the catalyst of a new syndrome, Trump Derangement Syndrome.

I will briefly discuss what a syndrome is and what the various contributing factors are leading to the development of TDS in our culture, as well as the ideological forces driving it forward. Additionally, a synopsis of several underlying psychological theories along with a few hypotheses will be presented.

Now let's have some fun before we start learning anything too serious, and please remember that generalizations are just that, and nothing more. So, no getting upset! Perhaps if you are too fragile, you should put the book down and walk away while you still have a chance …

Okay, now that they (the Democrats) are gone, let's get down to business.

So, it's June 2015, and Donald John Trump formally declares that he will run for office. For the observant person, you knew this was coming for some time. The writing was on the wall for years. His many politically charged comments, his continuous public exposure, unstoppable desire for name recognition, and his unwavering patriotism were some of the many tell tail signs that he desired the office of president. But I digress…. Back to June 2015. Donald Trump announces his intentions, and everyone goes crazy. People on the left, people on the right. He gets slammed by everyone! "This must be a joke," and "He just wants the publicity" and "He is damaging the Republican Party" are just a few of the statements we all heard after he announced during the Republican primaries of 2015.

He invoked fear among all, including the Republican Party. They knew he was not beholden to anyone, and that his unconventional nature may be just what the American people wanted. Someone that was willing to take a stand, to be American, and hold his head high in the face of opposition, regardless of party affiliation. I have to say, considering the verbal sparring that most of Donald Trump's competitors experienced during the 2016 primaries, the majority have accepted their beatings with grace and moved forward—including those he described as "Little Marco," "Low Energy Jeb," and "Lyin' Ted." They engaged him and lost. Perhaps they understood that the race to the presidency was a dog fight, a street brawl, or a donnybrook, but none of them could have anticipated the level Donald Trump would rise to because of his desire to become king of the hill.

His passion went unsurpassed. But the majority have accepted the bumps and bruises, most likely learned some valuable lessons, and will be back to fight another day. Most work with him now, not against him. As they realized, his style of fighting to be on top was not personal, but rather Donald Trump's tenacious nature was fueled by his overwhelming patriotism. His former contenders also have that same passion for their country and show it through their willingness to work with a man that held nothing back when running against them. This is where the Democrats fall short. Their inability to graciously accept defeat; their low self-esteem, or simply their sense of entitlement may be some of the reasons for TDS flourishing. So much of what we hear from Ms. Clinton is an endless list of excuses, sounding a bit like a spoiled child who didn't get her way.

The realization that Donald Trump was going to win the primaries was becoming evident to many. With that brought both glee and fear among the DNC. Those who were still mesmerized by the previous president and thought that liberal ideology and the Liberal New World Order would rule supreme for the remainder of time, were quite happy because they thought Donald Trump was a joke. However, there were some from the DNC that truly understood why Donald Trump was someone to pay attention to, and that realization created fear. This ignorance combined with fear once unleashed would become a maelstrom of hateful propaganda propagated by the left in order to maintain control of the government. The left wing liberal machine began to pick up steam, bringing various areas of society including the media, post-secondary educational institutions, and the world of entertainment including political commentators, sports figures, singers, and actors on board. By no means is that an exhaustive list of those that jumped aboard the train to hate Donald Trump, patriotism, the Stars and Stripes, and the American way of life. So, many of these people were whipped up into a frenzy, and once banded together almost seemed unstoppable. Groupthink had obviously come into play, and most of the left isn't sure when or where to get off the 'crazy train.' It basically became an excuse for people to act uncivilized, attacking people, destroying property, and shutting off their minds to any perspective that wasn't their own.

Donald Trump wins the nomination and shocks as well as pleases so many. It seemed to almost happen overnight; Donald Trump became a rock star! Well, to those that loved him at least. To his opponents he became the ultimate nemesis, although many denied his ability to successfully cross the finish line. But wait; it wasn't just the DNC that lacked confidence in Donald Trump. Many with the RNC were convinced that Donald Trump would simply be a drag on their agenda culminating in a loss at the 2016 ballot box.

I could easily identify several so-called Republicans that appeared outwardly displeased with Donald Trump winning the White House. I'm not sure if they were simply holdovers from the previous administration; if they hated Donald Trump because he was not a lifelong politician; feared that they would be exposed for some wrongdoing; were just left-leaning Republicans; were just simply jealous, or suffering from the initial stages TDS. Paul Ryan, Jeff Flake, Mitt Romney, and John McCain all come to mind … From where I sit, it was quite obvious that they did not want to help Donald Trump achieve his goals of draining the swamp. They were certainly proficient at dragging their feet, stabbing Donald Trump in the back, or blatantly opposing him outright. Are these actions of jealousy and fear, or simply symptoms of TDS? I would suspect the later.

The left, the right, the media, newscasters, entertainers—everyone—was dumbfounded by his success. And TDS was starting to spread. His rallies contributed to the flourishing of TDS by polarizing the American people more than ever before. He pointed out the ugly truth about so much and so many. Things that many were not comfortable hearing, but what others knew to be true. His rallies were unprecedented, attended by thousands, with even thousands more *wanting* to attend. The American people finally had a voice they understood. He was speaking their language, and they were responding.

We are all familiar with the phrases, "Build the wall," and "Lock her up." These phases will bring smiles to Republicans, but will make Democrats cringe. Both statements draw out intense emotions, no matter your party affiliation. Why? Well, there are several reasons for this including your political perspective and ideology. However, there are more deeply ingrained reasons, such as how, when, where and by whom you were raised; your personal experiences in life; and in general, how well you adapt to change and challenges. I will discuss and draw from several theories as I postulate the evolution of TDS and how it's on its way to becoming a true syndrome. This is not meant to be a text book, but rather to share a belief and expose the birth of a burgeoning syndrome. Plus, to have a little fun.

CHAPTER 1

WHAT IS TRUMP DERANGEMENT SYNDROME?

"A sick thought can devour the body's flesh
more than fever or consumption"

- Guy de Maupassant
1850-1893

Diagnosis is as fundamental to the field of medicine as it is critical to applying treatment and prognosis; it enables clinicians and scientists to communicate effectively—essentially to be able to speak the same language, and of course, it is necessary for conducting research. Mental disorders are considered to be under the umbrella of medical illnesses; however, historically they were considered separate entities and were under a person's control. The first official attempt to gather information about mental health in the United States was the recording of the frequency of "idiocy/insanity" in the 1840 census.[1] Using this broad classification today, the frequency would be off the charts!

As with all disorders, in order to understand an illness, you have to identify the symptoms. More formally, according to the current *Diagnostic and Statistical Manual of Mental Disorders,* Fifth Edition (the DSM-5) a mental disorder is defined as, "a syndrome character-ized by clinically significant disturbance in an individual's cognition, emotional regulation, or behavior that reflects a dysfunction in the psychological, emotional regulation or behavior that reflects a dysfunction in the psychological, biological, or developmental process underlying mental functioning." Put more simply, mental illnesses are health conditions involving changes in thinking, emotion, or behavior (or a combination of these). Mental illnesses are associated with distress and/or problems functioning in social, work, or family activities.

We have all heard the term Trump Derangement Syndrome (TDS) thrown around extensively over the last few years. So, what exactly is Trump Derangement Syndrome? First let's a take a look at the word 'deranged.' This often triggers imagery of Hannibal Lecter, the character portrayed by Anthony Hopkins, in the *Silence of the Lambs*, as well as the depraved character The Joker, portrayed by Heath Ledger in the movie *The Dark Knight*. The word *deranged* originates from the Old French word *desrengier,* which means to "disarrange, throw into disorder." More aptly defined, the *Cambridge Dictionary* defines deranged as "completely unable to think clearly or behave in a controlled way, especially because of mental illness." . . Completely unable to think clearly or behave in a controlled way indeed. *The Merriam Webster Dictionary* defines "a syndrome as a group of signs and symptoms that occur together, and characterize a particular abnormality or condition."

And, how do we define Donald J. Trump? At first blush, we can say objectively that he is a real estate mogul, businessmen, entrepreneur, American president, and patriot.

So, what is TDS? Various definitions have been floating around social media including one from Wikipedia that "Trump Derangement Syndrome (TDS) is a mental condition in which a person has been driven effectively insane due to their dislike of Donald Trump, to the point at which they will abandon all logic and reason." The *Urban*

Dictionary defines Trump Derangement Syndrome as, "A mental dysfunction causing those detractors with hateful thoughts and feelings about Donald Trump to go unhinged."

Based on the behaviors of those from the left and the liberal elitist, one can wonder: Have the American Democrats simply gone mad? Back in 2003 the psychiatrist and columnist Charles Krauthammer declared a new psychiatric syndrome, "Bush Derangement Syndrome: the acute onset of paranoia in otherwise normal people in reaction to the policies, the presidency—nay—the very existence of George W. Bush." At that time, this syndrome would have been considered more at a subclinical level; however, then Donald J. Trump decided to enter the political field, and the virus exploded to hysteric levels where individuals are now unable *to* distinguish between legitimate policy differences on the one hand and signs of pathology on the other. Dr. Lustig in his article, "This Is Your Brain on Trump," identified TDS as, "ostensibly a mental condition in which persons have been driven effectively 'insane' due to their dislike of Donald Trump to the point at which they abandon all logic and reason."[2]

TDS is so prevalent that it has become part of the American vernacular spoken in mainstream media, as well as by politicians and even the president himself. US Senator Lindsay Graham from South Carolina was quoted as saying, "Whether you agree with impeachment or not, Trump Derangement Syndrome has reached a new level. House Democrats refusing to send the Articles of Impeachment to the Senate because they don't like the way we may do the trial—that is just scary."[3] Florida Representative Matt Gaetz also during an impeachment hearing said, "I would suggest that you need to move on to issues that impact the lives of the American people, not your own politics and the affliction of your own Trump Derangement Syndrome," when addressing New York Congressman Jerry Nadler.[4] And the president retweeted a quote from journalist Trish Regan:

> "Diagnosis positive: @CNN is infected with Trump Derangement Syndrome. I'm calling out CNN for irresponsibly politicizing what should be a unifying battle against a virus that doesn't choose sides."[5]

Buck Sexton (@BuckSexton, January 9, 2020) said:

> "Blaming Trump for Iran shooting a civilian airliner out of its own airspace while committing an act of war against both America and Iraq-may be the closest we have come to isolating the virus that causes Trump Derangement Syndrome."[6]

How do you know if you've been afflicted by it? TDS columnist Howie Carr, offers the following checklist of symptoms characterizing Trump Derangement Syndrome (TDS).[7] He opines that you may have TDS:

- If you embrace all immigrants, legal or illegal—except Melania Trump.

- If you've posted on social media that 2016 was the worst year of your life.

- If you have attached a safety pin to some article of your clothing to indicate that you will provide a "safe space" for any of your fellow NPR tote-bag carriers so traumatized by what has happened.

- If you have blamed Hillary's loss on one or more of the following bogeymen: James Comey, the Russians, the electoral college, Islamophobia, homophobia, misogyny, voter ID laws, fake news etc., etc., etc.

- If you agree with the liberal law professor who had to cross to the other side of the street to avoid walking past a Trump hotel.

- If you want to see Trump's tax returns from when he was a private citizen, rather than those of the lifetime members of Congress who have somehow become multi-millionaires.

- You think the epic homeless crisis in California is Trump's fault, rather than the result of Dems and their liberal policies.

- You still do not believe the Trump economy was working (and Bidenomics is).

The illness appears to have infected the left like no other ailment. Psychiatrists have seen more Americans coming in to therapy complaining about angst over President Trump. An American Psychological Association survey shows just 26 percent of Republicans feel stressed over the political climate, compared to a whopping 72 percent of Democrats.[8] After the 2016 election, Cornell University recently hosted a "cry-in," complete with blankets, hot chocolate and tissues.[9] The University of Pennsylvania brought in a puppy and a kitten for therapeutic cuddling; Tufts University held arts and crafts sessions for students, and the University of Michigan Law School scheduled an event called, "Post-Election Self-Care with Food and Play," which included coloring, blowing bubbles, sculpting with Play-Doh, and positive card making.[10]

Hollywood and some of its predominantly left-wing actors have suggested that Donald Trump should be shot, beheaded, or assassinated etc., while others have suggested and even acted out on disclosing who in their world were/are Republicans in order to 'out' or 'shame' them. This is simply another form of bullying by the left against conservative beliefs. The actress Debra Messing called for a release of names of people in her industry who attended a Republican National Committee fund raiser in Beverly Hills. In a tweet she suggested that the *Hollywood Reporter* list all of the attendees. She wrote, "Please print a list of all attendees please. The public has a right to know."[11] This call for an outing of people based on their political leaning smacks of McCarthyism of the 1950's. The call to release the list of fellow actors who were Republicans and Donald Trump supporters, is with what I can only imagine was the hope of shaming them to change their minds on whom to support, or at least getting them banned from acquiring additional work in the industry, thereby ruining their careers.

The righteous and virtuous left have called President Trump homophobic, racist, fascist, Islamophobic, antisemitic and so on and so on … If you google Trump, the algorithms I'm sure are set on all things negative for Trump, and according to them there is no shortage! A so-called comedian held up a mock bloody, severed Trump head as a gag, and they have called for his assassination as a "joke," which is truly not funny.[12] Trump has been blamed for the shooting at the newspaper office in Annapolis in 2018, the Ohio train derailment of 2023, the baby formula shortage, the southern border crisis, the COVID-19 pandemic, the humiliating withdrawal from Afghanistan, the blackouts in Venezuela, and global warming to name a few. Anything and everything that happens bad in the world is Trump's fault to the exclusion of everything else. A blindness surely caused by TDS! What has caused this unusual, atypical response in a Democratic society which used to support differing thoughts and ideas without fear of retribution? In the next chapters, using psychological underpinnings, we will break down and define what, where, how, when, and who this new potential diagnosis is impacting.

CHAPTER 2

LOCUS OF CONTROL

Who Is in the Driver's Seat?

*"What separates the winners from the losers is
how a person reacts to each new twist of fate"*

- Donald Trump, 45th President of the United States
1946-

An important psychological principle that can drive our behavior is locus of control. Are you the author of your own destiny and driving yourself to where you want to head in life? Locus of control is a concept that helps give a better understanding behind what drives us, and if we are truly in charge of our own destiny, or if some other factors outside of our control are making things happen for us. In another sense, it dictates how much control we perceive to have over our own lives.

Julian B. Rotter initially introduced the concept of locus of control as a generalized belief in internal versus external control of reinforcements that arise from an individual's general expectations.[13] He postulated that an individual would tend to either believe that their life can be controlled through decision-making or that outside factors determine their path without them having any influence. Individuals who have an internal locus of control believe that the outcome of their actions are results of their own abilities, and that their hard work would lead them to obtain positive outcomes.

Those who have an external locus of control attribute outcomes of events to external circumstances outside of their control. People with an external locus of control tend to believe that the things which happen in their lives are out of their control, and that even their own actions are a result of external factors, such as fate, luck, or the influence of powerful others. Please keep in mind that we are not addressing faith or religious beliefs when discussing this topic and are rather strictly focusing on the construct of locus of control. Such a person tends to blame others rather than themself for their life's outcomes. Maybe the easiest way of describing the difference between internal and external locus of control is simply to think of something good or bad that happened to you in life, and try to determine if it was luck or hard work (or the lack of either) that brought you to that point. Basically, do you take responsibility for your own behavior or not. Interestingly, research has shown that people with an external locus of control tend to be more stressed and prone to clinical depression as compared to those with an internal locus of control.[14]

A number of benefits come from having an internal locus of control. Internals tend to live a healthier lifestyle by exercising more and making better food choices; by preparing better financially for potential financial crises; they cognitively stimulate their offspring more than externals, and tend to be less risk adverse.[15] Internals also tend to have more grit and perseverance when dealing with adversity. They usually proceed with going to work and maintaining their daily routine following a health shock or significant event. And along that line of thinking, internals reportedly search for employment more intensively when needing to do so.[16] Also, prenatal internal locus of control is positively associated with IQ of offspring. More specifically, mothers with an internal locus of control produced children with a seven-point higher IQ.[17]

In one such example of an internal locus of control, I will refer to a friend from the gym. He is an elite athlete who has participated in several high-level competitions. When he achieved first place, he attributed it to luck, rather than to the hour upon hour, day after day, and month after month of dedicated training and sacrifice over the years. He would say things like, "Those workouts were better suited to me," and "the other athlete must have had a bad day," or "I just got lucky." This is obviously someone that tends to exhibit an external locus of control. This type of person tends to place responsibility on outside forces, including other people for what has happened. Now if he would have alternatively said, "Don't think this comes easy, or I have lived my training for the last ten years and worked my ass off day after day, and sacrificed so many things to earn this," then he would have an internal locus of control. This type of person (an internal) is one who takes responsibility for their own actions; is less obedient and willing to challenge or resist social pressure, therefore not conforming to outside influence.

So, what do you think about yourself? Do you have internal or external locus of control? What are your beliefs about who or what is responsible for your life and the decisions made within it? Is there powerlessness over either important or unimportant events in one's life? Obviously, there are many varying degrees to this construct, and it is not a hard and fast rule, but rather an overall perspective of how things are perceived. Granted, there are certainly numerous external contributors to how one develops and evolves as they grow and mature, but is it not also how the individual interprets those inputs and deals with them in their own unique way that eventually shapes the person to become who they are?

For example, I am the product of divorced parents from the latchkey generation (aka Gen X), and was subsequently raised by my mother. As a young child, I realized that my parents had their differences, and that overall, it was better for everyone in the family if they were to separate (in a twelve-year-old's mind). I liked both of my parents, and held no animosity towards them for the breakdown of our family (although perhaps I should have), but that is for another day's conversation. I felt there was nothing I could do about their relationship failure, so I accepted the facts and moved on with my own life the best I could. Of course, there were many instances where having my father in the picture would have been beneficial to my development, but that was simply not viable any longer. As well, my mother worked extremely long hours to support us, and I surely would have also benefitted from her being home regularly, but again that was not an option, so I found ways to accept and deal with those issues. Now on the other hand, one of my older brothers struggled considerably with our parent's failed marriage. For years he would constantly blame our parents for his shortcomings, rather than accepting what had happened, learning from, and improving because of the event. Yes, of course their failed marriage had detrimental effects on me and my siblings. But locus of control played a factor in this scenario and how we all dealt with it. Can you see how one deals with events in their life can shape them positively or negatively, aka internal or external locus of control?

Now ask yourself, were you raised in a family supported by parents who worked for the government? Were your parents seasonal workers; did they own their own business; were they wealthy or poor; were they educated or not; did they believe in the American dream, or was that saved for someone else; was family important to them, or were they driven by something else; was their wealth no matter how much or little given to them, or did they earn it? These are some potential questions to ask yourself when considering the roots of your own locus of control. Obviously, there are a wide variety of potentialities of where each of you will land on the spectrum of locus of control, but if you give it a little thought, you can probably trace and identify a few of the roots of your own beliefs as they pertain to your upbringing.

Now, let's take a look at President Trump for a moment. This is a man who has had many ups and downs in his life, but he has never given up. The tenacity and resilience to succeed is what people see in him (aka internal locus of control). He is a fighter, and "one who is willing to fight for us!" His current and past behavior has spoken to people's instinct and judgment. Even to this day, his life seems to parallel an aggressive rollercoaster—president one day, getting a mugshot the next. His tenacity, perseverance, and his internal locus of control are certainly admirable.

When we examine those with an external locus of control, we can generally say that they believe they have an uncontrollable destiny. They most likely unwittingly describe themselves as being victims, where things happen to them and the victimization of so many things in their lives can be overwhelming. It is my belief that you—the individual—is responsible for where you end up in life. Certainly, there are extraneous influences that push and pull you in various directions, such as your parents, family, abilities at school, social support network etc., but it is how you eventually deal with those things that will show your true character. Granted, some of us are faced with more obstacles than others, and some of us have what others would deem an 'easy road.' Regardless, I have met some who appeared to have it all, and yet accomplish so little, while on the other hand I have met those who have had almost nothing and yet created greatness. The miracle of the human will … or will not.

An important factor is the family structure and how it can play a role in developing either internal or external locus of control. For example, one study found that large, single parent families headed by women tend to develop external locus of control. Moreover, children growing up in families where the parents have been positive, supportive, and consistent tend to develop internal locus of control.[18] These are but two examples of how one grows and evolves to develop in different ways. Stability and resources, family beliefs, reward for effort, and consistency in one's life can impact the direction one tends to go. That said, for some of us locus of control also tends to become *more* internal as we age, just as becoming a conservative usually comes with age. Interestingly, a saying commonly credited to Winston Churchill was first cited in a public 1872 letter from academic and politician, Anselme Polycarpe Batbie of France (who accredited Burke) and reads:[19]

> "Celui qui n'est pas républicain à vingt ans fait douter de la générosité de son âme; mais celui qui, après trente ans, persévère, fait douter de la rectitude de son esprit."

With the English translation being:

> "Anyone who is not a republican at twenty casts doubt on the generosity of his soul; but he who, after thirty years, perseveres, casts doubt on the soundness of his mind."

With the more well-known Churchill summation being:

> "If you are not a liberal at twenty, you have no heart. If you are not a conservative at forty you have no brain."

Numerous great thinkers have eloquently expressed their thoughts about the differences between liberals and conservatives. Even John

Adams, the second President of the United States had his spin on it declaring that:

> "A boy of fifteen who is not a democrat is good for nothing,
> and he is no better who is a democrat at twenty."

Perhaps it is because as we age, and if an individual is insightful, they gain wisdom, and have learned from past successes and failures. Therefore, they come to the realization that their choices have consequences, either positive or negative. Now, granted, a person can be somewhere in between regarding locus of control. It doesn't have to be all or nothing, one or the other. It could be a little of this, and a lot of that. So, many factors could lead you to your personal level of locus of control, and whether it is internal or external.

Unfortunately, there are those who don't come to the realization or state of maturation, and rather seem to find themselves in a perpetual state of victimhood. Individuals focusing on always having a "victim" mentality are much more likely to have an external locus of control.[20] In other words, they believe they are not in control of their own destiny, but rather some external force is pushing them in whatever direction they flow in life, leading them to feel like victims in perpetuity.

Researchers have also found that a tendency for interpersonal victimhood consists of four primary areas including the perpetual need for recognition of their victimhood, moral elitism, lack of empathy for the suffering of others, and persistent rumination about perceived prior victimization.[21] Strangely, this type of person tends to believe that they are superior, and view themselves as being better than or above all others due to their misguided perception of being morally pristine and elite. Having this grandiose concept of oneself, allows them to comfortably look down upon others, and to judge and condemn them for "inferior behavior." This moral supremacy is then wielded like a magic wand to destroy anyone of their choosing. If they label you with some sort of -ism after deciding that you were immoral, you will be condemned.

Now you may wonder where this elite attitude comes from; well in my opinion, it is born out of the ineffectual, those who are attempting to hide their own inadequacies. I have found more times than not, people who are overly aggressive, angry, or extreme in one way or another, are typically trying to hide something about their character. They tend to dismiss, justify, or even feel entitled to their own aggressiveness, all the while projecting it onto others. Ask yourself: How many times have I witnessed the political left claim something against the right, only to later be guilty of the same thing they were claiming. If you want to know what the left is up to, just listen to what they are saying everyone else is guilty of doing. This behavior known as projection, and is a form of defence mechanism incorporated by the subconscious as a protecting factor of the perpetrator's id, ego, and superego according to Sigmund Freud. Freud's daughter Anna, went on to further study projection and described it as one of human's primitive defence mechanisms, which she defined as, "Attributing one's own maladaptive inner impulses to someone else."[22]

By projecting these negative concepts and hurling insults and accusations, they typically succeed in bringing down their opponents because, after all, they are the "morally elite." Preoccupied with their own victimhood, this superiority and lack of empathy for others' negative experiences eludes them. They are so enthralled with feeling sorry for themselves that they cannot or will not try to see things from a different perspective, and therefore are unwilling to accept responsibility for their own negative behavior.

But, don't be frustrated by those inflicted with moral elitism, as that way of thinking generally stunts growth and has contributed greatly to the development of Trump Derangement Syndrome, which I will expand on more when I discuss moral development. Not surprisingly, political ideology and locus of control have been correlated in research. While the research has been somewhat limited in scope, the results certainly reflect what I would have suspected. Take a moment before reading on, and think about what I have been saying so far. Then ask yourself who would more likely be registered as a Republican, and who would more likely be registered as a Democrat? Not a surprise, right!

In the 1972 U.S. Presidential election, research of college students found that those with an internal locus of control were substantially more likely to register as a Republican, while those with an external locus of control were substantially more likely to register as a Democrat.[23] These findings were replicated in 2011 and 2014.[24] Republicans have been found to have an internal locus of control, and Democrats an external locus of control. Not suggesting one is better than the other—well maybe I am—but either way, this is simply fascinating. And it demonstrates why the Democrats canvass college and university students so aggressively. Youth typically brings naivety, malleability, and liberal ideology, especially regarding world views, and when coupled with professors who are generally left leaning in their beliefs and teaching methods, these same youth are perfect targets for acquiring votes for the left.

I was going to conclude my chapter here; then Hillary Clinton's voice reminded me once again that she appears to exhibit an external locus of control. The number of excuses she has made for losing the 2016 election is unfathomable. It was everyone's fault except her own, according to her. However, I certainly understand her frustration as I suspect she obviously had a lifelong plan culminating in her becoming the first female US president. Her life was likely planned out quite strategically to achieve that goal, and with amazing success, except for a few hiccups along the way, including Donald Trump's 'army of deplorables'.

I can hear you ask: What about President Trump not accepting defeat? Well, I have said Hillary was complaining with no evidence to the contrary. There is ample objective evidence to the contrary to support Donald Trump's claims. Voter fraud has been associated with globalists, so-called anti-fascist groups, politicians, as well as the average corrupt citizen. Ballot stuffing, intimidation of poll watchers at polling stations, faulty voting machines, excessive mail-out ballots, unmanned ballot drop boxes, deceitful media propaganda, and dead people voting have all been suggested and factored into the belief of a corrupt 2020 election. I will take a deeper dive into these issues later in the book.

We have demonstrated that external locus of control is more prevalent in the liberal mindset of individuals like Hillary Clinton and that she appears to be part of a larger cohort which encompasses millennials and Gen Z as well as their parents, teachers, and professors. These groups are not only some of the many who suffer from TDS, but they are also responsible for the aggravation and propagation of TDS. Those who care about our freedoms should take advantage of our internal locus of control and effect change in a positive way to save our country from the idealists that pontificate their moral supremacy.

CHAPTER 3

MILLENNIALS AND THE PARENTS WHO RAISED THEM

Who Dropped the Ball?

Hard times create strong men
Strong men create good times
Good times create weak men
Weak men create Hard times

- G. Michael Hopf, Author
1970-

D onald Trump represents what the left fears most, a threat to their 'under the table, backroom dealings' that have been part of the corrupt establishment for generations. His desire to "drain the swamp" has motivated the left to plant the seeds of TDS into those individuals referred to as the "useful idiots" by Retired US Secret Service Special Agent and conservative commentator Dan Bongino. The propagation of TDS has flourished due to the perfect environment, whereby the liberals assisted in planting the seed, with it taking root, and branching out through the millennials.

A large proportion and one of the driving forces behind the birth and growth of TDS are the millennials and their parents—Yes, the generation that was thrust upon the traditional working world between the early 1980s and roughly the millennium. These individuals have many needs and desires, but little effort beyond throwing tantrums and manipulation to achieve their desired outcome. This generation has been shaped by the exponential acceleration of the dependence on ever changing technology. They were raised by cosseting parents where praise and adoration was indiscriminately dispensed at every turn, and that was coupled with constant rewards for little or no accomplishment within a regulated and controlled environment both in the home and school.

As I mentioned in Chapter 1, I tend to generalize, so if you are a millennial or a parent of one, please read this with an open mind. I am aware that there are exceptions to every rule including the stereotypical notions regarding millennials of being lazy underachievers who are overly sensitive. Contrary to that stereotype, I personally know a number of millennials who are wonderful, productive, and very successful individuals. And you know who you are! Heck, there is even a movement among some in the younger generations who are just killing it, like Ben Shapiro, Candace Owens, and Charlie Kirk. I digress …

Unfortunately, the traditional descriptions of millennials are rooted in the numerous examples where the stereotypical behavior abounds. It is the needs of this cohort—which is the largest generation in American history, yes even bigger than the Baby Boomers—that has contributed greatly to TDS.

In a recent study cited in *Forbes Magazine* by Zack Friedman, it was determined that at least 50 percent of millennials and to a slightly lesser extent, their younger counterparts, Gen Z, are planning to move back in with their parents after being on their own.[25] Yes, planning to do it! It was noted that a number of these individuals have no shame in living with their parents until the age of 28 … Yes 28! A good portion add that they will likely live with their parents until the age of 30. Debt was reportedly a major factor behind this decision derived mostly from student loans as well as other over spending. These cohorts don't appear to take personal responsibility for their spending, most likely because they are funded by someone else, typically their parents.

Perhaps if a student could not afford the school they attended, they should have found a less expensive institution; held a job to supplement their living costs and education, or simply stayed at home while attending school so as not to incur room and board costs from the educational institution. Perhaps foregoing the spring break vacation; buying a ridiculously over-priced pet; or spending endlessly on prepared and delivered food and drinks? These are generations that have no concept of what it is like to sacrifice, and would rather reap the benefits of other's labor while lounging in their pajamas. The concept of an honest day's work is simply not understood, nor accepted, or is vehemently denied out of sheer laziness. Immediate gratification is all they know. It was how they were raised; get whatever you desire, along with a constant stream of praise. It is no wonder that they are gullible enough to believe Joe Biden when he proclaims that he will pay off all outstanding student debt, presumably in exchange for a vote ...

They are not to be held solely responsible for their behavior as their parents are also at fault for these substandard achievers. The individuals who have morphed into the classic millennial, have most likely been reared by the so-called Helicopter Parent—the parent who is ruthless on their mission to provide their child with whatever whim they desire regardless of who they lay in waste on their quest to keep little Johnny or Suzy happy. The over-the-top pandering to their children's needs has led to the downfall of a generation, one that is fraught with depression, anxiety, and obesity. Research has shown that high helicopter parenting has been linked, "to low mastery, self-regulation, and social competence, and to high depression."[26] This type of parenting has a significant impact on the child's ability to manage their day-to-day activities including personal relationships. They may exhibit regulatory issues and adjustment problems in response to life's demands because their parents' coddling has left them lost in the world with no concept of how to Improvise, Adapt, and Overcome, which of course is one of the unofficial mantras of the US Marines. I suspect the stereotypical millennial will never become a Marine. These fierce warriors are individuals who are prepared for any challenge through their desire and ability to overcome obstacles in their path. They are always faithful, always forward, and are what I suspect to be the polar opposite of a stereotypical millennial.

The fragility that the Millennials and Gen Z exhibit has evolved over many years, and will therefore take considerable time to undue. They are not solely to blame for their behavior because it typically stems from the style of parenting that they have been exposed to. We have all heard the rhetoric regarding millennials and have chuckled under our breath. Growing up, they were fawned over in a society where everyone gets a medal for participation; picks their own grade at school; or has three birthday parties a year. Dr. Gummer states that "Children need rules, boundaries and opportunities to feel the cold, go hungry and fall down and hurt themselves, so they can learn from their mistakes."[27] Perhaps the parenting of this generation was suited more to accommodate the parent's life than to teach their children true life lessons.

The helicopter parenting style is detrimental to children, but has validated the perception, 'I want, therefore I deserve' to blossom. Now I certainly won't say that these parents were trying to harm their children. That would be ridiculous. On the contrary they were most likely trying to improve their children's chances of success in the world. This 'assistance' can and often does continue into adulthood, with a helicopter parent becoming so intertwined with their child's life that it often appears unnatural. I wonder what Freud would say … But seriously, think about the College Admission Scandal of 2019, which involved thirty-three wealthy individuals who engaged in fraudulent behavior by manipulating, lying, or bribing their children's way into prestigious educational institutions.[28] These knuckleheads paid over $25 million in total to William Rick Singer between 2011 and 2018 to do their dirty work by bribing school officials and inflating test scores. We all know the actresses among others who were involved. This is obviously an extreme example of helicopter parenting, but it certainly gets my point across regarding how far some parents will go to please their children. A 2015 study by University College London tracked more than 5,000 people since birth.[29] It found people whose parents had intruded on their privacy in some way—encouraged dependence—were much more likely to be unhappy in their teens, thirties, forties and later on in life.

The millennials are now adults, but they can still be seen as lacking maturity, adaptability, resiliency, or growth because their parents have not provided them with any of life's necessary lessons. They are everywhere in society trying to control their environment via cancel culture. It is sad that they have not learned some of life's basic lessons. I remember one of the simplest and most meaningful things we were taught when growing up. It was a child's rhyme that went like this …

"Sticks and stones may break my bones,

But names will never hurt me."

Now, I am sure most of you remember those words or at least a variant of such, but unfortunately, they have been lost somewhere along the way over the last forty years or so. The rhyme is obviously intended to limit physical retaliation by teaching resiliency, and it is a defense technique against verbal harassment and bullying. Name calling, teasing, bullying—whatever you want to call it—is wrong, and can be incredibly detrimental to the recipient, and should be curtailed as much as possible. But, as we all know, there are people in this world—no matter their age—who can, well … be obnoxious. That is exactly why it is a parent's responsibility to teach their children resiliency, so their children can grow up to become happy, stable, well-balanced individuals.

However, in today's world, children are shielded from all day-to-day negative experiences which in turn teaches them to be overly sensitive when confronted with difficult situations. This is an unrealistic approach outside of a utopian society. For example, when a parent or teacher tells a student that, "It makes me sad to see you two argue and say hurtful things to each other because you both are wonderful, and I love you, so please be kind to each other because when you fight, we all have hurt feelings and feel bad inside. So, please be happy and kind to each other, hold hands, and be friends, okay?" That all sounds great, and it is nice to see children forgive each other and make up, but … what it also does is to negate their experience of current negative emotions and feelings. This focus on positive emotion over any other has likely led us to where we are today in that children being taught in that way don't know how to internalize and deal with the more negative emotions of anxiety, fear, anger, and hate. Parents and educators need to realize that it is alright for children to experience failure and sadness on occasion as it brings value and helps to fill their toolbox for later on in life. This teaches children how to be resilient, which is such a valuable ability during their formative years and beyond.

Resilience is defined as the process of adaptation in the face of adversity, trauma, tragedy or other sources of stress such as family and relationship problems, health issues, or workplace stressors. Or for the purpose of this discussion, the loss of a presidential election. As much as resilience involves "bouncing back" from these difficult experiences, it can also involve profound personal growth. As previously mentioned, for example, after the 2016 elections, Cornell University hosted a "cry-in," complete with hot chocolate and tissues for disappointed Hillary Clinton supporters.[30] The University of Pennsylvania brought in a puppy and a kitten for therapeutic cuddling. Sounds more like what someone might do for children in kindergarten who are nervous about being away from home for the first time. And more recently parents are hiring and paying hundreds of dollars an hour to so-called professional cuddlers to comfort their adult children while they attend college!

The exhibited need for therapy in this circumstance, no matter the form, is evidence that these generations are lacking the ability to deal with disappointment on their own. Parents find it necessary to integrate some form of assistance. This development is true evidence that TDS is becoming more prevalent in society to the degree where it needs to be formally addressed by professionals. These sufferers of TDS exhibit a lack of ability to adjust to situations that make them uncomfortable, and is paramount in demonstrating the development and spread of TDS.

Author, Kristin Tate, stated that "This is an extreme reaction from millennials who are being forced to come to terms with the fact that we have a president that they don't like—this is what losing feels like. We are grooming our students to be sensitive crybabies when we need to be showing students how to deal with world situations and how to be adults—there are no 'safe spaces' in the real world."[31]

The helicopter parents' removal of obstacles in their children's pathway relieves the youth from the opportunity to learn from challenges starting early in life. If as a child you don't learn to compete, win, lose, accept criticism, come in second, third, or even last place, getting 50, 60, or 70 percent on a project, or learning to work in a team environment—how in the world will you be able to do those things happily as an adult? Chances are you won't, and you will likely melt as you are a mere 'snowflake.' Mainstream terminology to describe the youth of these generations is 'snowflakes,' which I believe to be an appropriate use of nomenclature. *Collins English Dictionary* (describes a snowflake as a derogatory term toward a person who has an unwarranted sense of entitlement, inflated sense of uniqueness, and one who is overly emotional, self-entitled, easily offended, and unable to accept differing views from their own. Yep, sounds like a snowflake.[32]

This inability has led many to try and make this group more comfortable by adjusting language used while in their company. This is once again accommodating their fragility, and denying them the opportunity to grow and mature. It's certainly not to say that these individuals are totally weak, especially in today's world where they have a sense of communal action (groupthink) through various social platforms on the internet, and is also where they have demonstrated the willingness to 'deplatform' those that make them uncomfortable. Where would they be without the anonymity of hiding behind their computer screens with their 'thousands of friends'? This so-called deplatforming technique that they incorporate is a type of political activism against free speech used by individuals or groups to basically shut down someone they perceive to be controversial or who makes them uncomfortable. So rather than engaging someone in an intelligent conversation with an opposing view, they will simply have a tantrum or bully others to get their way and avoid having a constructive discussion which might allow them to find mutual ground or understand alternate perspectives.

It all comes back to how they were raised. Their behavior has likely been reinforced by their parents throughout their lives. And now as young adults, believing they are the center of the universe, they are exhibiting this same inflated sense of ego and disregard for their fellow citizens. This cohort has been described as being overly self-absorbed, and narcissism levels have risen 30 percent as compared to previous generations.[33] Even the Chinese Virus Covid-19 did not deter them. Once bars, beaches, and restaurants opened, and protests and riots took place, the number of those infected with the virus exploded within that cohort. It's simply a matter of selfishness, which is ironic because this is also the cohort that claims to care so much about the world, sustainability, the environment, and their fellow man. They are the generation of virtue signaling … but talk is cheap.

As a colleague once suggested, perhaps this parenting style comes from the guilt of having both parents working and not having someone (either parent) home to care for their children. I can relate from having been a latchkey kid. I can understand why a person would want to give more to their children after having not spent time with them, but it is a terrible mistake. One of the most important things you can give your children is your time. Trying to buy them off or allowing them to misbehave will not result in the best outcome for anyone involved. This overindulgence is similar to how children can be raised in a split household. I am getting way off base here …

Daniel Wesley, founder and CEO CreditLoan.com, points out that instead of saving for the future, millennials place more importance on experiences such as taking a gap year, distant vacations, or living in large, expensive cities. Recent studies show that millennials are more likely to travel on a whim for example to Europe, whereas their older counterparts, the Baby Boomers, would plan far in advance for such a trip, which is a great example of immediate versus delayed gratification. Again, they seem to be asking: "Why would you pay your own way if someone else is standing behind you willing to pick up the tab? (Especially when you haven't been taught self respect and independence.) Perhaps your well-to-do friend, your parents, or a paternalistic left-wing government is willing to be the safety net, if only for a while until they move on to the next bleeding-heart victim.

The demands of millennials for safe spaces, gender neutrality, a politically correct environment and concern for so-called micro-aggressions has blossomed into a left-wing bouquet of chaos and a tool to condemn anyone who disagrees. Most rational individuals will acknowledge that the awful behaviors of sexism, racism, radicalism or any other 'ism' have no place in our society. Unfortunately, there are those who will manipulate others' behaviors and words to instigate or sow division and tension using those isms.

The evolution of the PC culture has spread well beyond the generation I was just addressing, and the culture has found a foothold in countless arenas including popular media and culture, universities, public institutions, and the political world as well as those who report on it. This spread and acceptance of PC culture is most likely due to the ease of manipulation of those with whom one disagrees—thus praying on the vulnerabilities of those who are generally good-natured individuals.

Social media platforms are even starting to censor what people are posting including President Trump on numerous occasions if it doesn't fit their narrative of what is acceptable. Not surprisingly, these platforms are heavily staffed with … you guessed it, millennials! The arrogance and intolerability exhibited by these individuals while hiding behind the anonymity of the internet is extreme. They claim to want the world to be a better place, but it seems they believe that their 'version of better' is the only option. Unsurprisingly, the individuals who are comfortable living in their parent's basement or sleeping on a friend's couch are the same people who are promoting a socialist's lifestyle where hard work is not necessary to receive an income.

Now that I have slammed millennials, I am sitting here wondering how and why some people in older generations have millennial ideology. Perhaps they simply never grew up? Maybe they found it too difficult to leave the safe confines of the university campus and became professors? Everyone knows the old adage by George Bernard Shaw, "those that can do, those that can't teach." Or maybe, they came from either a privileged background where money wasn't something to worry about or perhaps an underprivileged background where they learned dependency on government or others to take care of them.

However, most millennials are without an agenda aside from condemning others. In order to fill the void they experience, a number of them attempt to draw on social movements of the past, calling them their own in order to feel accomplished. They do it now using the internet to assemble a group to protest, as it is much easier than it was say in the 1960s or 1970s feminist and counterculture movements. The so-called protestors of today are merely copycats of true revolutionists of bygone days. They have no true agenda and therefore attempt to steal what they find idealistic in order to give their own lives some sort of meaning and accomplishment. It is what I call *plagiarism of the soul*, which identifies deep-seated problems that are not addressed within the liberal psyche and can culminate into a grieving phase as they lack insight regarding what they are experiencing.

This lack of agenda is most likely derived from their sense of the world around them being uncontrollable. Their minds have been numbed by the belief that the world has a pre-subscribed plan, and that they are not accountable for their actions, good or bad. Due to lack of independent thought, it seems they have no desire or motivation to set goals. They have been denied by being raised in a sheltered environment shielded from any harshness or adversity which has led to them becoming void of true passions and emotion. This insecurity has inspired them to piggyback off of previous cultural experiences at best, and more likely has driven them to simply complain about others in order to make their mark in the world. This overwhelming tendency to blame and criticize rather than engage is how those with TDS have attempted to deal with the election loss of 2016 through avoiding accountability and justifying their feelings by placing responsibility on external forces.

CHAPTER 4

THE STAGES OF GRIEF THROUGH THE DEMOCRAT LENSES

"In the struggle for survival, the fittest win out at
the expense of their rivals because they succeed in
adapting themselves best to their environment."

- Charles Darwin, Naturalist
1809-1882

I t became clear that when President Trump was elected in 2016, those who were suffering from TDS began to experience grief as a result of their loss at the ballot box. To illustrate my point, we can use the Kubler-Ross model of the stages of grief, which includes Denial, Anger, Bargaining, Depression and Acceptance.[34] The amount of time each person remains in each stage varies considerably, and an individual may not go through the stages in a fixed progression, but they may jump back and forth between the stages during the grieving process.

Stage 1 is Denial. Denial is essentially a common defense mechanism used to protect oneself from the hardship of considering an upsetting reality. It's your brain saying, "There is only so much I can handle at once. It can't be true. This is not happening!" The grieving process can be stalled by replacing it with unrealistically inflated hope that things can change, and it can still be salvaged. It can be seen as the initial paralysis upon hearing the bad news. Once the suppressed feelings surface, the healing process begins.

Stage 2 is Anger. This is a common and necessary stage of grief. Anger is a normal and necessary response. Initially, individuals may not be able to connect with their feelings of anger, with the unknown, evoking fear and dread. Fear, at that point, trumps anger … pardon the pun. This is when you think, "Why is this happening to me?" and you might blame others. When anger eventually sets in, it is because you have let go of some of your fear. Redirecting your anger towards family and friends is common.

Stage 3 is Bargaining. This is the stage of false hope where you believe you have some measure of control. You are willing to do anything to avoid accepting that it's over. The negotiation could be verbalized or internal and could be social, or religious. You may say, "Please God, I promise to do better if …"

Stage 4 is Depression. This is perhaps the most understandable of Kubler-Ross's stages, as depression is commonly associated with grief. This is when the individual comes to terms with the fact that the situation is not going to change. This is a time for reflection, but may lead to hopelessness, self-defeat, and blame. A liberal may make statements such as, "The world is coming to an end," or "It's anarchy." In this stage, you might withdraw from others; you may feel numb, like you are living in a fog. Life may feel overwhelming.

Stage 5 is Acceptance. In this stage, you have come to terms with your new reality and have adjusted. When acceptance occurs early in the grieving process, it can feel more like surrender. Your emotions are more stable, and you feel you can move forward. At this point the good days tend to outnumber the bad days.

Okay, so let's start at the beginning. Donald Trump announces and everyone denies his seriousness, abilities, and chances of being chosen in the primaries, let alone his chances of becoming president in 2016. The denial and arrogance were unprecedented when listening to the left-wing media explain how there was no way for Donald Trump to get nominated as the RNC representative, to win a debate, to reach 270 in the electoral college, and that *'everyone'* was shocked and surprised that he won. Half of the voting population of the United States of America voted for Donald J. Trump, so why in the world do they continue to say things like, "No one expected him to win?" Denial, that's why! Reporters and commentators have said things like, "It is shocking" and, "It was an earthquake," and "It seemed impossible" after Donald Trump was victorious. Shear denial at its finest hour. The first stage of grief involves the drive to know why, which becomes consuming and can come at the expense of rational thoughts and behaviors. "How could Hillary have lost? How could this have happened? She was ahead in the polls! Everyone said she was going to win. It can't be true. This is not happening!"

The media's denial has grown exponentially dysfunctional, denying all of President Trump's accomplishments. Their distaste for him runs so deep and is so transparent when reporting on him or his opponents. Consider the simplest of things like gushing over people such as Joe Biden, Barack Obama, or his wife Michelle Obama. For example, whenever they speak about Michelle Obama, you will typically hear comments like how wonderful, beautiful, or poised she is. But, to the contrary, those comments are rarely if ever spoken by the left wing media about Melania Trump, and this is a woman who made a career based on her appearance. She started modeling at the age of sixteen years; was signed by an agency in Milan at eighteen, and worked in some of the major fashion centers of the world including Paris, Milan, and New York earning a living based on her appearance. Additionally, she appeared in several magazines, and she has been on the cover of *Harper's Bazaar, Vanity Fair, GQ, Sports Illustrated,* and others.[35] Sounds to me like it would be natural to address her appearance and compliment her regarding her poise and appearance as First Lady. Denial. Denial. Denial. I can only imagine why they don't like her. She appeared to be declared persona non grata, seemingly guilty by association, I suppose.

Tech guy and owner of the Dallas Mavericks, Mark Cuban heatedly proclaimed that there would be a stock market crash; there would be "huge, huge" losses, and basically the world would come to an end if Donald J. Trump were elected.[36] I was surprised to see someone who was so successful, behaving in such an acrimonious manner. Contrary to his claims my tiny trading account certainly smiled when Donald Trump won the presidency. TDS was likely clouding Mr. Cuban's judgment and common sense. I suppose being skilled in the tech world doesn't equate with someone understanding human nature. Perhaps it is more a reflection of his animosity toward Donald Trump, or his denial that Donald Trump may achieve something that he himself may have wanted to attempt but simply never had the kahunas or capability to do? He has indicated interest on several occasions, stating that he, "Could beat both Trump and Clinton," but has never officially thrown his hat into the ring. What's that saying? Oh yeah, "Shallow brooks run noisy." Regarding my trading account, it sure has been struggling since Joe Biden landed in the White House.

Well, then there is Hillary's denial … we all know that too well. The one hundred excuses of Hillary Clinton. Sounds like a good book to read for a laugh! But again, you can smell the denial and desperation on her from a mile away, and see how it has led to a generation not accepting the election results of 2016. Clinton has pinned her loss on several different factors, such as how journalists covered the election, former FBI Director James Comey, and how the questions were asked at the debates (even though she was provided ahead of time with substantial information regarding the questions by Donna Brazile, the Democrat strategist).[37] I guess 'strategist' could be perceived as another word for cheater. Here are fifteen reasons Hillary says she lost.[38] There are many more that would fill this book, so we decided to cap it at fifteen.

1. Russia: "What Putin wanted to do was…influence our election, and he's not exactly fond of strong women, so you add that together and that's pretty much what it means."

2. The DNC: "I'm now the nominee of the Democratic Party. I inherit nothing from the Democratic Party. It was bankrupt…I had to inject money into it – the DNC – to keep it going."

3. Sexism and misogyny: "Sexism and misogyny played a role in the 2016 presidential election. Exhibit A is that the flagrantly sexist candidate won."

4. A Democratic predecessor: "It's really difficult to succeed a president of your own party who has served two terms. That is a historical fact."

5. Bernie Sanders: "His attacks caused lasting damage, making it harder to unify progressives in the general election and paving the way for Trump's 'Crooked Hillary' campaign."

6. Wikileaks: "The Comey letter, aided to great measure by the Russian WikiLeaks, raised…doubts again. And so even though I won the popular vote, enough people in a few states…were just raising all these questions."

7. Her "traditional" campaign: "I was running a traditional presidential campaign…while Trump was running a reality TV show that expertly and relentlessly stoked Americans' anger and resentment."

8. The debate questions, not being asked, "how the candidates planned to create jobs": "I was waiting for the moment when one of the people asking the questions would have said, 'Well, so, exactly how are you going to create more jobs?'"

9. Political journalists: "[Journalists] can't bear to face their own role in helping elect Trump, from providing him free airtime to giving my emails three times more coverage than all the issues affecting people's lives combined."

10. Campaign financing: "You had Citizens United come to its full fruition. So unaccountable money flowing in against me, against other Democrats, in a way that we hadn't seen and then attached to this weaponized information war."

11. President Obama: "I do wonder sometimes about what would have happened if President Obama had made a televised address to the nation…warning that our democracy was under attack. Maybe more Americans would have woken up to the threat in time."

12. TV coverage of the campaign: "When you have a presidential campaign and the total number of minutes on TV news was 32 minutes, I don't blame voters. Voters are going to hear what they hear…and if they don't get a broad base of information to make judgements on."

13. Low-information voters: "You put yourself in the position of a low-information voter, and all of a sudden your Facebook feed, your Twitter account is saying, 'Oh my gosh, Hillary Clinton is running a child trafficking operation in Washington with John Podesta.'"

14. Women under pressure from men: "They will be under tremendous pressure from fathers and husbands and boyfriends and male employers not to vote for 'the girl.'"

15. James Comey: "The determining factor was the intervention by Comey on October 28 … but for that intervention, I would have won.

To the liberal mind, Donald Trump triumphed by error, by accident, by Hillary Clinton's own fault—forgetting to campaign properly in Michigan, the same way that you might forget to fasten a window and … damn it … you let a burglar in. These are the tantalizing, "What-ifs?" of history that keep us all living on a knife's edge. What if James Comey hadn't announced that the FBI was looking at some emails related to Hillary Clinton just days before the election?

Anger is the second stage in the grieving process. Anger can be described as the response to feeling hurt, injured, or wronged. We might believe that we are to blame, or finger pointing may occur. When we feel our world is out of control, we try to control the things we can. So, when I reflect on the rioting and tearing down of statues, looting, violence and random crime etc.—for which there are far too many examples to list—I realized that the majority of the left had entered the second stage of grief, which is anger. Initially, individuals may not be able to connect with their feelings of anger, thereby evoking fear and dread. When anger eventually sets in, it is because you have let go of some of your fear.

In the days following the 2016 election as soon as the election was lost, I watched coverage on several networks. On one such broadcast I saw Van Jones, a CNN news commentator; once the election results were called, and he pronounced that this was representative of a "whitelash," and continued to say various negative things about Donald Trump and his supporters.[39] It sounded a bit racist from where I sat, but those on the left would never be divisive or racist, would they … hmmm (!). Does Mr. Jones think that no people of color voted for

Donald Trump? Why is he discounting them? To place all Republicans into some sort of group that dislikes or hates everyone who is not white sounds very narrow-minded, bigoted, and racist. Other subtle evidence of anger and backhanded attacks includes the language used through subtle linguistic juggling. Regarding the use of "Mr. Trump" to address the president by many media outlets as compared to appropriately saying "President Trump," ask yourself: How many times has the previous President Barack Obama or the current so-called President Biden ever been disrespected to such an extent while in power? Liberals have been heard saying in the same conversation, while referring to President Trump as "Trump," and to the current or previous presidents with the more respected salutations, without any correction or admittance of fault. Unless of course you are comedian Kathy Griffin. I think she skipped denial and went right to anger. This was clearly depicted in her jihadist style photo posing with a bloody mask of President Trump's severed head. That was wrong on so many levels. The optics weren't great, triggering images of Hamas and ISIS-type behavior.

Over the last few years, exhibitions of anger have been expressed by the general masses evidenced in all of the rioting and looting by the Democrat minions. Their anger has hit several flashpoints when trying to stop conservative speakers from presenting and actually managing to have them cancelled on numerous occasions. Anger has been displayed by looting and destroying property to the degree where major corporations are shutting down and leaving the Democrat-run cities and towns. And anger has been displayed through grotesque physical attacks against unwitting victims, many times ending up in severe injury or even death.

How about John Kasich, the former Ohio Governor, staying in the primary race well beyond any chances of him winning the nomination?

In 2018, reflecting back on Kasich's run for the presidency; he indicated that it was the media that had the greatest interest in him being nominated, not actual supporters who could cast votes. His refusal to accept defeat, and what looked to be anger directed toward Donald Trump appeared obvious. His anger years later is still evident. During a CNN interview, Kasich not only said that the, "President was flailing; he is in a meltdown, and that his base was fraying and shrinking."[40] He added that Donald Trump had created a 'brand' problem for the Republican Party, indicating that a number of his supporters would jump ship, and say, "I was never a part of this, and I never supported him." And he seemed to blame Donald Trump's supporters for enabling him to continue to do all the misdeeds that the left keeps claiming he has done. Then he, along with Utah Senator Mitt Romney actually spoke at the 2020 DNC National Convention against Donald Trump. Yes, I said DNC! That really should not be a surprise to anyone as they are obviously RINOs. The bitterness exuded from both of these men is palpable when it comes to Trump. Especially with Kasich, who was trounced in the primaries after working for years making connections and 'playing the game' to become president, and as a person who has often insinuated that he is smarter than most around him. To be bested by a newbie in the political world ... that must have stung! Well, I guess he is still feeling the burn and is looking for retribution years afterwards. After all he surely presents as a 'Never Trumper.' Romney was the lone Republican to vote to convict Donald Trump during the Senate's impeachment trial of 2020.[41] What a piece of work! Can't say I'm shocked that he is coming out against the president today. While a few appear to still be in the denial or anger stage, I feel that this is a mischaracterization of their appearance and behavior.

Now it is not exactly the perfect representation of Sir Isaac Newton's

Third Law, but I feel that it is applicable in today's world. He formally stated that, "For every action, there is an equal and opposite reaction."[42] What some might describe as *bystander apathy* or *low-grade depression*, I would suggest is better described as silence to achieve a desired outcome or a 'reaction.' The left wing politician's inaction has led to incredibly destructive actions across the country. These behaviors of denial and anger continued through the presidential election of 2020, and if President Trump is victorious in 2024, we will likely witness denial and anger once again, but I expect it will occur much sooner and on a larger scale after the election than we observed last time. The third stage of grief is bargaining. Bargaining occurs when denial breaks down, and we start to acknowledge reality, but we're not ready to give up the illusion that we still have control. Basically, we try to compromise to find an easier, less painful way out. During the stage of bargaining, an individual may ask for a spiritual leader, and begin praying to change the outcome. You are willing to do anything to avoid accepting that it's over. The Democrats would rather see the United States fail than have President Trump succeed. They would rather have the economy nose dive than admit that President Trump's policies were successful. Talk show host Bill Maher is a man whose aversion to all things Trump almost rivals that of actor Robert De Niro. Maher actually said the following words as he articulated his desire to remove the President from power: "I feel like the bottom has to fall out (of the economy) at some point, and by the way, I'm hoping for it. I think one way you get rid of Trump is by crashing the economy. So please, bring on the recession. Sorry if that hurts people, but it's either root for a recession or you lose your democracy."[43]

What a selfish piece of work! That guy is a multi-millionaire who makes his money off of the middle-class viewers whose finances would be destroyed by a recession. Rather than see the world moving towards peace under President Trump, Democrats like him would likely have rather seen the failure of the denuclearization negotiations with the supreme leader of communist North Korea, Kim Jong Un.

We have heard comments like, "Well he can't run again after this," and "four years and counting," and, "How much damage can he do in four years," and "in less than four years, we can get a Democrat in office." At this stage, you are willing to do anything to avoid accepting that it's over. Fast forward to the Biden presidency and look where the world stands; Russia invades Ukraine; Hamas strikes Isarael; the Middle East is heating up once again; Palestinian terrorist supporters around the world are attacking US embassies and spewing hatred towards Jews; and it seems very likely that China will make its move on Taiwan. But even with all that going on, the left wing ideological machine would still rather make some sort of bargain to accept Biden's shortcomings than admit that Donald Trump was a better president than ineffectual Joe. Then, if Donald Trump wins in 2024, within the near future after that, you will hear reports about people becoming depressed, as they realize four years won't go quite as quickly as they expected; that he is still ruining the country and the previous president's accomplishments, and that a woman or person of color should be president. This will be a time when the individual comes to terms with the fact that the situation is not going to change. In the *Washington Times,* I just read an article about the entertainer Cher complaining once again. She reportedly vows to leave the US if Trump wins in 2024 and that, "I almost got an ulcer the last time."[44] I guess she didn't like the thriving economy, low unemployment across all demographics, and the fact that the US had not entered any new wars, etc., under Donald Trump. Evidently, she would rather have the looting, violence, division, and new wars on the horizon that Joe Biden has managed to govern over the last couple of years.

Joe Biden announced his intention to run again in the 2024 election, or should I say that the team behind Biden just announced his intention of running. For some time, it was obvious that Joe Biden would be the chosen nominee for the DNC to run against Donald Trump, and I say that loosely, "Run against." There was very likely a grand plan implemented by the deep state to put forth a candidate that they could push around and control. However, I do believe that the same deep state actors have a plan to replace Joe at the DNC Convention in August of 2024 with a more viable candidate.

All the while Hillary Clinton has been likely trying to find some way of weaseling her way back into the presumptive driver's seat, to only once again be humiliated by Donald Trump. I can just see Hillary Clinton with her hands up Joe Biden and Kamala Harris' asses, running them like hand puppets, and making them spew the traditional Democrat playbook. No wonder the two of them sound confused; it's actually Hillary trying to do two voices at once … "Root causes …" and "You Lying Dog-Faced Pony Soldier …" Back to the stages of grief. Sorry about getting side-tracked there. I tend to get carried away with humorous thoughts as my passion on these topics is tremendous. There is just so much to say….

OK, to the last stage of grief: acceptance. Acceptance doesn't mean you condone what happened, but it simply infers that you are no longer trying to change the past, or things over which you have no control. Hillary and the others seem unlikely to reach this stage while Donald Trump is still in the picture because she lost the election and he made a mockery of her. When acceptance occurs early in the process, it can feel more like surrender, which the far left would never submit. Hillary and the others are unlikely to reach this stage while President Trump is still in the picture to any degree. They may feel a sense of acceptance as a *have* to, not because they *want* to. One can only wonder had Hillary been a mature role model to the left and graciously accepted the results of the election, would the left have exhibited the childish tantrums, crying, and continued denial of the Democratic process over these last years? There are currently some signs (one year prior to the 2024 election) that some have come to accept the fact that Donald Trump was a great president, just as they will come to realize what a mess has been made since Joe and Kamala moved in.

The acceptance will take longer for others, and for many, they may never get there; however, I suspect history will shine brightly on Donald Trump, as it shines on those who fight the good fight, and those who make the tough decisions. Generally, those with the greatest moral character are remembered favorably. Time will tell when academics can look back at the hard numbers and see who produced positive results as the President of the United States.

All of that being said regarding the five stages of grief, I still believe there will be a resurgence of denial, anger, bargaining, depression, and acceptance throughout his campaigning and term if Trump is elected again in 2024. I don't believe many who suffer from TDS have yet reached the acceptance stages of grief, as they appear to be stuck in the second and third stages cumulatively. The anger and bargaining are still quite evident in their behavior. Once the 2024 election unfolds, there will be the moment that those who are suffering from TDS will either go into remission or move forward into the more advanced stage of depression followed by acceptance. The remission will likely only occur if Donald Trump is not re-elected, thereby eliminating the deep concerns of the key TDS antagonist. If he is to win in 2024, after what is expected to be an extreme resurgence of violence and rioting, we will likely see a shift in behavior toward bargaining, depression, and acceptance, with the latter highly unlikely until many years after he leaves office.

The grieving process can be stalled by replacing it with unrealistically inflated hope that things can change and it (the presidency) can still be salvaged. I believe many liberals are trapped in this phase. Stalled. Unable to move forward. They are hanging on to the hope that President Trump will be found guilty of collusion, conspiracy, obstruction, or any of the nearly 100 potential BS crimes, despite the fact that there has been *no* genuine evidence after years of investigation. It feels like we have been watching a page out of the Salem Witch Trials. Their 'Plan B' to criminally charge the president is based on absolutely no wrong-doing. It is transparent and obvious to everyone that the motive is to stop him from running and winning again. It smacks of desperation! This is only broadening his base as everyone can clearly see him being railroaded. They have already impeached him twice, once over a phone call and the second with incitement to insurrection (come on, really?) but ultimately, he was acquitted. The Constitution defines justification for impeachment if "treason, bribery, or other high crimes and misdemeanors" have occurred.[45] It's an audacious notion, but the Democrats continue with these unrealistic condemnations. On the one hand, they say they want him to run as they will easily beat him over any other opponent, and yet on the other hand, they find despicable lowlife DA's, prosecutors, and judges that will attempt to extinguish the president's hopes of ever being in office again. These so-called justice warriors are disgusting, and they are only pursuing this cause in order to fulfil their own sad, pathetic, low self-esteem and weak egos under the guise of cultural Marxism. The real question is: Will the strategy of Republicans evolve rapidly enough to push back to keep the party and democracy alive?

CHAPTER 5

MORAL DEVELOPMENT

The Good, the Bad, and the Ugly

"The pendulum of the mind oscillates between sense
and nonsense, not between right and wrong."

- Carl G Jung, Psychiatrist
1875-1961

Perhaps it is the lack of moral development and poor judgment that has stifled the ability of the fanatical left to naturally graduate through the stages of grief. Paralysis is leading them to make irrational decisions.

Piaget, Erikson, and Kohlberg were leaders in their field and exceptional students of human development and behavior. Each had a different focus. Jean Piaget studied intellectual development. Erik Erikson focused on emotional development, and Lawrence Kohlberg was interested in moral development. I realize that you are not reading this book to get a lesson in the history of psychology, so I won't go too much farther down that path. Fittingly for this conversation, Kohlberg is the only naturally born American of the three theorists I mentioned above, and he addresses moral development, which is something that appears to be gravely lacking at the higher stages in today's society.

What is morality and moral development? Morality can be described as the principles or beliefs that some behaviors are right or good, while others are bad or wrong. Making choices between the good and bad will shed light on your morality. It has been suggested that morality is developed over time, and that one passes through stages as they become more moral. Moral actions can be very different depending on who or what your belief system is. Can we not make assumptions about theories of morality, and to whom they are relevant? What I believe to be a moral action, you may feel is immoral and vice versa. From terrorists and waterboarding, to Mike Bloomberg spending over 1 billion dollars in four months during a presidential bid, a Brookings article asks, "If money can't buy you votes, what can it buy?"[46] Where does one draw the line on what is morally acceptable?

Kohlberg broke down moral development into six stages beginning in childhood through to adulthood.[47] He grouped them into three phases graduating from one level to the next as you grow/develop/evolve in your thinking regarding justice, and which continues throughout an individual's life. He suggested that not everyone reaches the higher levels, and that one climbs through the stages in order. Kohlberg focused on the reasoning behind one person's decision versus another's if placed in the same circumstances. In other words, how would you react in a particular situation as compared to how your sibling, neighbor, teacher, or any other person would react in that same situation. A basic question of moral development could be related to driving the speed limit. Does one not speed because they don't want to get penalized by receiving a ticket and having to pay a fine, or does one not speed because they understand the inherent potential of not only harming themselves but also that of another person. Moral reasoning is a necessity of ethical behavior. Therefore, he postulated that the farther one progressed through the stages of moral development, the more capable they were of more moralistic decision-making.

The three phases include Pre-Conventional, Conventional, and Post

Conventional with each being broken down further into two stages each. For the purposes of this discussion, I want to discuss the last two phases that primarily encompass adult development.

The second phase is the Conventional Level. The conventional level of morality is typical of adolescents and adults who internalize moral standards. An individual's sense of morality is increasingly based on interpersonal relationships. At this level, children continue to conform to the rules of authority figures. But, although they understand that there are conventions dictating how they should behave, following the rules is not necessarily related to the prospective punishment. Above all, they wish to ensure good relationships with others.

Within the Conventional Level, are stage three, Conformity, and stage four, Law and Order. During the Conformity stage, children's actions are motivated by the approval of others. Morality arises from living up to the standards of a group such as family or community. Older children will often do their best to be good members of a group. Their moral decisions are based on whether they would win the approval of individuals whose opinions matter to them. The intentions of their actions are important regardless of the outcome. In the Law-and-Order stage, a person accepts rules because they are important in maintaining a functional society. Rules are the same for everyone, and it is essential that all members of society obey them. Moral reasoning goes beyond the need for individual approval of the Conformity stage. Instead, morality is being determined by what is best for *most* people. Individuals who obey law and authority and don't challenge the established social order are perceived as being good.

According to Kohlberg, most individuals don't develop their reasoning beyond this fourth stage of moral development in which morality is still predominantly dictated by external forces. He indicated that only 10-15 percent of the population is capable of achieving the Postconventional Level of moral development because the sense of morality is defined in terms of abstract principles and values. Those individuals who attain the highest level of moral development question whether what they see around them is good. There is an increasing sense of individuals being separate entities from society. Morality on this level comes from self-defined principles. Laws that are seen as unjust should be removed or changed. Disobeying rules is not necessarily wrong when they are incompatible with personal principles. Within the postconventional level is stage five, Social Contract and stage six, Universal Ethical Principles. Individuals at stage five of moral development understand that society is full of contrasting opinions and values that should be respected. Laws are regarded as flexible social contracts. Laws that are not in everyone's best interest should be changed to meet the needs of most society members. In this context, morality and individual rights take precedence over established laws. In the last stage of moral development, Universal Ethical Principles, individuals construct their own principles of morality that may conflict with society's laws. Moral reasoning has become more abstract and relies on universal, ethical principles including equality, dignity, and respect. Laws are valid only when they are fair, and unjust laws can and should be disobeyed. Kohlberg maintained that not many individuals could consistently operate at this level.

In psychology and philosophy classes, moral dilemmas are often used to help people think through the reasoning for their beliefs and actions. When confronted with a decision about the right thing to do in a particular situation, there may be a good reason *for* it as well as *against* a choice, and the individual may have to make a less wrong or more right decision. Facing this type of dilemma can be incredibly conflicting to a person's core principles and values. Making choices can be so stressful that a person may freeze and be unable to make a choice. But, that in itself becomes a decision, which also may in itself become even more burdensome. Just for fun, let's do a couple of exercises and see where you land. One of the most widely recognized moral dilemma questions in the field of psychology was created by Kolhberg.[48] He proposed the Heinz dilemma. No … This has nothing to do with ketchup.

It is presented to make one think about choices they might make and the reasoning behind those choices. The explanations you give, will help determine where you land on Kohlberg's stages of moral development. So, here it goes:

> A woman was on her deathbed. The doctors thought one particular drug might save her. It was a form of radium that a druggist in the same town had recently discovered. The drug was expensive to make, but the druggist was charging ten times what the drug cost him to produce. He paid $200 for the radium and charged $2,000 for a small dose of the drug. The sick woman's husband, Heinz, went to everyone he knew to borrow the money, but he could only gather about $1,000, which was half of what it cost. He told the druggist that his wife was dying and asked him to sell it cheaper or let him pay later, but the druggist said: "No, I discovered the drug, and I'm going to make money from it." So, Heinz got desperate and broke into the man's laboratory to steal the drug for his wife.

Here is the question posed to you:

> Should Heinz have broken into the laboratory to steal the drug for his wife? Why or why not?

I would suggest that if you find the question intriguing, stop reading now and ponder the question; get a pen and paper and jot down your answer/answers including the reason for your decision. Afterwards, you can go online and look up the potential responses and see where you fall on your moral development as described by Kohlberg. Please keep in mind that many theorists including Kohlberg himself have stated that most people will likely never reach the highest stages of morality. Remember. This is just a fun exercise, so no getting down on yourself. Kohlberg suggested that the importance for the response lay in the *justification* offered, not simply whether Heinz should or should not steal the drug.

There is actually a similar real life story concerning Martin Shkreli dramatically increasing the price of a drug called Daraprim which his company Turing Pharmaceuticals produced.[49] It is important to hear all sides of the story before passing judgment.

Here are a couple more dilemma-based questions to ask yourself to get the brain juice flowing:

You are on a cruise, and all of a sudden something happens, alarms sound, and it is time to evacuate. The ship is going down, and you scramble along with several other passengers to get on a lifeboat. After entering the water, you look around and yours is the only lifeboat that made it into the water. And someone points out that the lifeboat is taking on water because it is overloaded. Another survivor points out that there are twenty-one people in the lifeboat that has a capacity of twenty. What do you do? If twenty-one people stay onboard, the lifeboat will sink and chances are everyone will die. Do you volunteer to get out of the lifeboat? Do you ask someone else to get out? Take a vote? If you ask someone, who is chosen? Hey, this reminds me of the final scene in Titanic! I suppose Jack didn't think there was enough room for him next to Rose on that piece of wood. Therein lies another dilemma. Go watch the movie again, and tell me who was more moral in that scene?

Now, let's get a little darker, and really test what people are capable of. As if it weren't stressful enough being on that lifeboat! Imagine you are in charge of an intelligence agency information gathering team, and have discovered a plot to kill thousands, no, let's say millions of people. What would you be willing to do to stop that from happening? I can almost hear you saying, "I would do anything." But, is that true? Are you truly capable of doing anything, and if so, could you live with yourself afterwards? Or on the contrary, could you live with yourself if you did nothing, and the outcome was catastrophic where millions died because of your inaction? These are incredibly difficult questions to answer honestly. You may already have an idea of what I am alluding to here. Some years ago, post 9/11, the CIA captured a few terrorists from the Middle East that had been involved in the brazen assaults against the US which sadly led to the death of thousands on American soil. It was determined that information pertaining to future attacks existed, and obtaining that information would be helpful in deterring future attacks. So, how far does one push the envelope of morality when attempting to obtain information to save lives? Will simple questioning suffice, or will advanced interrogation techniques be implemented, or do more drastic measures such as waterboarding, controlled fear, or sleep deprivation that drill down on a person's primal instinct for survival come into play? So, in your lead position, let's say as a psychologist, do you use every tool in your toolbox to extract the information from that person, regardless of possible detriment to their mental and or physical well-being? Or on the other hand, if you don't use all of your tools, perhaps many more die. What is the moral thing to do? Now, by no means am I either condoning or denouncing the activities that took place regarding these individuals. I am not so virtuous that I dare judge what took place; nor do I have all of the facts that unfolded in that situation. However, it is my understanding that some of the techniques that were used in obtaining required information were if not the same, very similar to what a number of enlisted individuals go through during SERE (survival, evasion, resistance, escape) training while in the US military. John Jessen and James Mitchell are two such psychologists that assisted in developing what have been described as 'advanced interrogation' techniques.[50] These techniques were put into practice for an extended period of time, and in my opinion likely continued to be used until the necessary information was gathered. Subsequently, the contribution these men made to the field of interrogation (good or bad) has been condemned, and they have faced investigations and lawsuits being filed against them for their participation. Eventually a US District Judge successfully encouraged all parties to arrive at a settlement before going to trial in 2017, so a 'legal' determination of their morality never actually took place.

Now, I will discuss a few situations regarding moral behavior that more closely relate to our current situation in politics and societal unrest, and I want you to be the judge in determining if these actions are moral or not. Michelle O … in her new book described feeling repulsed during the inauguration of President Trump, stating, "I stopped even trying to smile."[51] Or how about coming out three months before the 2020 election stating that she has, "low grade depression" … "Not just because of the quarantine, but because of the racial strife, and just seeing this administration, watching the hypocrisy of it, day in and day out, is dispiriting."[52] Now I'm not going to say she does or doesn't have low grade depression. But I can certainly identify what I believe to potentially be BS. Remember the card game Bullshit where people try to fake/bluff their way to a win? Calling Bullshit was how you could catch someone trying to sneak something past everyone to win. Well, I call *bullshit*! Please keep in mind that the following is pure speculation on my part. The timing in relation to the election was suspicious, but her use of the words, "racial strife and quarantine" raises flags. Had she recently been on a trip and returned from a high-risk area? Maybe she visited their new $11million home in Martha's Vineyard, although I don't believe that is a high-risk zone? Had she been in contact with someone who had COVID-19 symptoms? I am sure that would have been all over the news, if that were the case. So, ask yourself, why would she be "depressed" because of a quarantine that she was not required to undertake? That's right. Because in my opinion it's BS. My impression is that she used the pandemic as a reason for her depressive symptomology but also wanted to debase the Trump administration quite unfairly as he was working diligently to address the pandemic for all Americans. I suspect that she along with her husband pulled out all the stops to appeal to and manipulate the general public in an attempt to pull votes in what can be described as an "early October surprise." This in my opinion was their attempt to manipulate the public to gain sympathy and votes at the ballot box.

Similarly, regarding moral development, or more precisely, the lack of that development, I reflect on Joe Biden's appearance while campaigning for 2020, and well into his presidency as well as his current situation. He certainly looks to be in decline physically as well as cognitively during the many times an appearance has been covered by the media. Even from the early days of his sporadic campaigning, you could see something was awry in his physical demeanour; the puffy and vacant look on his face; the significant trouble with his word-finding ability along with stumbling up stairs, getting lost on stage, and falling off his bicycle, just to name a few things. Now I am not saying that his moral development is in question in this argument. I am saying rather the actions of the people around him including his family and associates is questionable based on what we have witnessed. I would like to think that if I were struggling in this respect, that my family, a good friend, or business associate would take action to protect me, at least from making a fool of myself like he has.

Perhaps this has been undertaken, but it just looks as if no one cares enough for this man to convince him to step down from what must be an exhausting and stressful endeavour, and which has likely been exacerbating his current health struggles and leading toward a much quicker decline. It is just sad! I suspect the people around him are so power hungry—and likely benefitting from his position—that they are willing to throw this man to the wolves to achieve the ultimate goal of bringing down President Trump. They hate Donald Trump that much, and glaringly displays how their TDS symptoms have clouded their judgment. Where is the morality in the people closest to Joe?

What about Hillary Clinton? Do you think she has any moral fortitude? Hillary Clinton on the run-up to the 2020 election, proclaimed that, "Joe Biden should not concede under any circumstances, because I think this is going to drag out, and eventually I do believe he will win if we don't give an inch…We've got to have a massive legal operation, I know the Biden campaign is working on that."[53]

Think back to the 2016 election night … I know you were all watching things unfold, just as I was. Do you remember when John Podesta, Hillary Clinton's campaign manager, made an announcement addressing supporters in New York extremely late in the evening of the 2016 election at 2:16 a.m. on November 9 stating, "We can wait a little longer," and "We are not going to have any more to say tonight," and "Head home. You should get some sleep. We'll have more to say tomorrow."

Clinton was nowhere to be found by her supporters or the cameras. This in my opinion was an attempt at a couple of things. First and foremost, I believe the outcome was an unbelievable hit to Hillary Clinton's ego, and a total shock to most in the DNC, not to mention all of the left leaning voters, pollsters, and media that had constantly been proclaiming there was no way for Donald Trump to reach the 270 electoral vote threshold; therefore, they needed time to recover and try to compose themselves before addressing the public. More importantly, I believe there was a scrambling attempt to avoid acknowledging their defeat to the public; to find some way to discredit the results and Donald Trump, just like how the they had belittled him during the run-up to the election. However, I also believe the biggest reason behind these statements had a childish, immoral, and vindictive purpose, which was simply to not give Donald Trump, his family, the RNC, and his supporters the satisfaction of a true victory and celebration that evening. My reasoning behind this is based on the simple fact that by 2:40 a.m., apparently Hillary Clinton called the Trump campaign to concede. Less than twenty-five minutes earlier, her campaign manager was telling people, "We have lots of time." "Votes to be counted." and that "We are not going to have any more to say tonight." This demonstrates a lack of maturity and moral development, from my perspective.

Many in the mainstream media are no different in their apparent lack of morals. The endless attacks that are incredibly trivial in nature, and in which on so many occasions are total misrepresentations of what the president has said. It seems that so many individuals are simply on a quest to confront and "catch him" at something, just anything, so they can say, "See, I told you he was a bad man." For example, when discussing Trump's view on immigration, hysterical TDS victims assume there is no difference between the president-elect's rhetoric (get out!) and his proposed policy (deporting known criminals who are in this country illegally).

As Reince Priebus, Trumps chief of staff, said, "He's not calling for mass deportation." He said "No, only people who have committed crimes."[54] The left, has so shamelessly, been putting on display their lack of moral development to a greater extent. They have said things like they are going to "blow up the system," and "burn down Congress," while supporting terrorist groups. For example: A tweet by Reza Aslan, an Iranian-born writer and television host living in America, stated when referring to nominating a replacement justice for Ruth Bader Ginsberg: "If they even *try* to replace RBG we burn the entire f-----g thing down."[55]

He later responded to the Senate Majority Leader of the time Mitch McConnell's vow to hold a vote on President Trump's nominee for the position of Supreme Court Justice, "Over our dead bodies, literally," Aslan tweeted.[56]

That kind of poorly developed morality, especially when in a position of influence, is frightening in my opinion. Aslan is regarded as 'some kind of religious scholar,' and he is promoting violence and using profanities to do so. Surely makes me question his intentions. Does he respect his fellow American that has welcomed him into the country? Why in the world would anyone on either the left or right listen to a person promoting such aggressiveness and violence? What he tweeted certainly doesn't promote the kind of society I want to live in. Aslan reminds me of a sore loser, a child who is not getting his way. I remember once when I was an adolescent playing a board game, and one of the players was losing to the point where he knew he could not win; he grabbed the board and flipped it into the air so no one had a chance of proclaiming victory. It seems as if the Democrats are willing to burn down the entire country so they can rebuild it in their own new world vision versus the iconic concept of the melting pot and American Dream where people have aspired to be for generations, and where everyone has the opportunity to lead a fuller richer life according to ability and achievement. Aslan, the so-called scholar, should be using his words for good instead of promoting the destruction of American society which people from around the world envy.

Rashida Tlaib, the US Representative from Michigan, is no different when promoting aggression and supporting Hamas in the Middle East.[57] Hamas has been designated as a terrorist organization by numerous countries around the world including the United States of America. In October of 2023, a series of coordinated unprovoked attacks, led by the Palestinian Islamist militant group Hamas resulted in the torture and death of over 1,000 babies, children, women, and men. She claimed that Israel had bombed a Palestinian hospital after evidence came out to the contrary. Ignorance plus ideology, equals violence. It simply makes no sense to have someone like that in government in what should be a civilized, rational society. Talk about a lack of morals!

On the other end of the spectrum, I recently listened to Jonathan Isaac, the Orlando Magic forward stating after not kneeling and actually standing for the flag and anthem during a pre-game event like a true American. And please keep in mind that this young man was the only one on his team to not kneel, which takes courage, confidence, and conviction. He stated the following when addressing the disrespect to the country when others have displayed angst regarding racism in such a manner:

"I don't think that kneeling or putting on a T-shirt for me, personally, is the answer. For me, Black lives are supported through the gospel, all lives are supported through the gospel," Isaac said. "We all fall short of God's glory, and at the end of the day, whoever will humble themselves and seek God and repent their sins, then we could see our mistakes and people's mistakes and people's evil in a different light, and that it would help bring us closer together and get past skin color, get past anything that's on the surface that doesn't really deal with the hearts of men and women."[58]

Mr. Isaac's ideas are worth listening to. He has obviously reached a higher level of moral development than a considerable number of people who are much older than he, and who have and do hold positions of power. He understands the importance of looking below the surface, into a person's character and history, and their willingness to state the truth and stand up for what they believe in. This approach is much more beneficial to our society as a whole. Certainly, it is easy to feel comfortable and content when accepted into a group, such as a team, a school, a state, a race, or a culture. So why is it that so many want to splinter off into smaller groups? Why not be proud to be Americans? Then, everyone regardless of color, religion, creed, etc. would be in the same group. I'm getting off base here again ... my apologies. All I am trying to say is that a number of people of color love and have fought for this country, and they acknowledge that it is disrespectful to refuse to stand. Individuals with grievances should simply find a better way to articulate their message.

Then there is Kentucky Attorney General Daniel Cameron. This man did an exemplary job conducting himself when relaying information about a high-profile case regarding a police shooting of a black woman.[59] He was condemned by so many on the left. He was disparaged and denigrated by many, and even called a sellout to the black community. Tamika Mallory, an organizer of a Women's March, called him a "sellout Negro" and said that, "He was a coward" and, "We have no respect for you, no respect for your black skin."[60] Please keep in mind that those particular statements are coming from a person who supports Louis Farrakhan, someone who hates just about everyone. That says a lot about her moral compass! Regardless of how ignorant the statements are, she has a soapbox on which to stand and deliver these vile statements spreading hatred. What do you think about her level of moral development?

I realize that I have given a number of examples of people perceived to be exhibiting less than ideal moral behavior. By no means do I think questionable moral behaviors are exclusive to Democrats, but the tendency for Republicans to be more conscientious certainly gives me hope that some people are still able to make rational common-sense decisions. Even when researching publications written within my field, I see a significant bias toward the left's moral high ground. The constant condemnation of the right no matter how subtle or slight seems to be sewn into just about every article or conversation I engage. There seems to be a sense of safety; perhaps it is grounded in the groupthink mentality. When listening to the news, searching online, reading the newspaper, or even when researching journal articles, there is usually some sort of underlying, backhanded insult directed at conservatives.

Anyone can see that there is political discord in America, as well as in many other regions around the world. Left against right, liberal against conservative. When consuming left wing media, it seems that most of the time, it is steeply slanted toward the moral superiority of the left, and is suggestive that it is the right who are the extremists lacking in moral clarity. This is even the case in 2020 when so many liberal towns and cities were being stained by left wing ideological bullies. The denial of the left's destructive behavior is almost laughable. Hopefully, at some point our shared beliefs on morality, decency, and respecting our fellow man—as well as what is truly right and wrong—will bring everyone back to center in order to have constructive dialog moving forward. Globally, things appear to be shifting toward that direction as recently in countries like Italy (Giorgia Meloni), Argentina (Javier Milei), New Zealand (Christopher Luxon), and the Netherlands (Geert Wilders) where conservative, common-sense leaders have been elected.

Interestingly, there has been recent research conducted by Hatemi et al., political scientists from Pennsylvania State University, suggesting that it may not be morals that shape one's political ideology, but rather the political ideology that shapes a person's morals.[61] What a great philosophical question! What came first, the chicken or the egg? So, let's take a closer look at this hypothesis. On the surface it certainly makes sense. How could anyone with morals promote transgressions against individuals of an opposing political party in a presumably moral country? The lack of rational discord, and tendency to act out aggressively in some form surely points in the direction Hatemi suggests. The-end-justifies-the-means mentality. But, are these truly conscious decisions, or are they actions born from the subconscious mind? Let's hope that Hatemi is wrong regarding which comes first. As if that is the case, democracy is likely doomed because it seems the pendulum of immoral behavior and hatred toward the opposing parties only appears to swing farther with each party's succession. Perhaps our common sense, humanity, and—yes—morality will be sufficient to stem the insanity we are currently witnessing. As I would suspect, at some point we will wake up and realize that some political leaders are so power hungry, they will do anything to conscribe followers into their destructive mobs. And perhaps that is why we are seeing more leaders like Donald Trump arrive on the global stage.

During Donald Trump's presidency, there was an unprecedented economic boom where he improved the employment rate across all minorities to record levels, with family incomes rising well over $5,000 per household.[62] He also lowered taxes across the board, made the USA a net exporter of energy, and kept fuel prices low for Americans. He mobilized resources to defend the southern border to keep Americans safe. Is it moral to continue to condemn Donald Trump despite his success and his true desire to improve the quality of life for all Americans?

The desire to condemn a man who has done so much for every facet of his country, has continued with blind rage that seems unprecedented. I believe one of the primary forces behind this TDS-driven rage is the catalyst—envy. Next, we discuss how this primal emotion leads to irrational, unjustified, and erratic behavior.

CHAPTER 6

ENVY AND NARCISSISM

Seeing Green

"envy is pain at the good fortune of other's"

- Aristotle circa 350 BC

Envy is typically born out of low self-esteem, neurosis, an insecure personality, and general feelings of inadequacy. It is a complex, social emotion which can impact our relationships, and can be summed up as wanting someone else's so-called advantage or posses-sions, either material or perceived. The envious individual may have the need for the desired attributes of another person to be taken way, or discredited, or the envious person may deny the desired attributes even exist in the other person.

The root of envy is the lack of self-satisfaction. However, in some cases, envy can work in a person's favor, if they use it to set and achieve goals for themselves—they may emulate a trait, striving for something similar in life. I want to be like….

German philosopher Friedrich Nietzsche suggested, "Look at who we envy; that is the person you should aim to be."[63] But again, I refer back to one who has an internal locus of control, one who believes they are in control of their own destiny. Nietzsche expressed that there was nothing wrong with envy, and that it could reveal a lot about oneself if they looked inward, allowing oneself to push toward fulfilling one's own desire. Envy can be a motivator of sorts. However, if one has low self-esteem, or an external locus of control, envy usually takes a more negative direction. It can manifest to the point where one experiences malice toward another for their perceived attributes, successes, possessions, etc. For example, one might be envious, and therefore want another's perceived physical prowess, charisma, or achievements, etc., and these thoughts can subsequently become overpowering. Envious feelings or desires can lead one to act in a malicious, spiteful, or even dangerous way if the feelings become too strong or uncontrollable.

Donald Trump has been the perfect target of envy for many. Hell, the guy has his own plane … hard not to be envious, right? As a man, he is envied for his many successes including being a real estate developer, notoriety, wealth, and what appears to be a close-knit family, all the while seemingly impervious to those who want to bring him down.

Once Donald Trump announced that he would be running for president, "The fangs came out" from so many sides, which was certainly predicated on envy and fear. The left, the right, the media, newscasters, entertainers, everyone was dumbfounded by his success and appeared so envious, they couldn't see straight. TDS was starting to spread further and further, and his haters acted crazier with each passing day. Perhaps they were simply holdovers from the previous administration, but so many seemed to envy as well as hate Donald Trump because he was not a politician. They feared that they would be exposed for some wrongdoing, or be left leaning Republicans. Paul Ryan, Jeff Flake, Mitt Romney, and John McCain all come to mind. From where I sit, it was quite obvious that they did not want to help Donald Trump achieve his goal of draining the swamp. And they were certainly proficient at dragging their feet, stabbing Trump in the back, or blatantly opposing him. Are these actions because of envy, jealousy, fear, or simply a culmination of TDS symptoms? I would suspect the later. I could point out numerous occasions where the left has cherry-picked statements to make the right look bad simply for the purpose of generating anger between the parties in order to mitigate rational discourse, and to further divide the electorate/the American people of all races, colors, and backgrounds.

As the president, Donald Trump is envied for having an incredibly long list of triumphs. He has the admiration of more voters than any other president in US history; he fulfilled his campaign promises; created a positive growth economy at twice the pace of his predecessor; reduced unemployment to historic lows; increased wages and wealth for almost everyone; restored pride in the country; achieved energy independence and engaged in superior foreign policy. These succusses fly in the face of all the naysayers, creating envy, jealousy, and anger toward Donald Trump.

There are those who respect someone who has achieved a lot in life, and then there are those who want to knock those people down. The latter may be attributed to weak character, low self-esteem, and/or envy. These factors are contributors that have inevitably led to our witnessing the development and evolution of TDS. For example, someone like Letitia James, the Attorney General of NY ran on the promise of convicting Donald Trump; she has pursued a civil fraud case against him and his corporation, seemingly over feelings of envy.[64]

She even went on a public rant, making vile statements inciting hatred against men, white people, and the elderly by proclaiming her hatred toward the Trump administration stating that it was:

"Too male, too pale, and too stale."[65]

President Trump was accused by Letitia of overvaluing his Mar-a-Lago estate in order to obtain a better borrowing rate from a lending institution. The courts ruled that his property in Palm Beach, Florida is only worth $18 million. Do the research yourself online, and you will clearly see how absurd that estimation is. Even before the trial began, the left wing lunatic judge Engoron ruled that Letitia had 'proven' that Trump's financial statements were fraudulent. Despite expert witnesses testifying to the contrary, indicating that his financial statements were in fact accurate and legally airtight. As well, Deutsche Bank in their testimony described President Trump as a financial whale, but regardless of all these facts, Engoron stripped President Trump of his ability to do business in New York and fined him more than $350 million for what clearly appears to be victimless non-crime.[66] It is simply outrageous and smacks of a narcissist mentality, lacking in moral clarity, wanting the focus of their envy to be stripped of his attributes, by using what looks to be a totalitarian police state to achieve a desired outcome. Letitia seems to have a misguided and uncontrollable hatred toward her perception of what the Trump administration represents. Her comments surely sound to me like a misandrist (think misogynist but against men), racist, and ageist. How can a person that does not like men, whites, or older people hold public office? And, what is wrong with the press, just ignoring those statements? Moreover, her attendance at Donald Trump's trial, even though she is not prosecuting the case, seems odd, given that one would assume someone in her position has a full calendar. I suspect her behavior is motivated by her envy and jealousy. Maybe she is envious of his wealth, his address on Fifth Avenue, or maybe she is secretly waiting for Donald Trump to ask her out on a date … LOL! Typically, that kind of anger and vindictiveness is rooted in low self-esteem, a neurotic insecure personality, or the feelings of inadequacy in the envious person.

As discussed above, some narcissists want those they envy to lose what they have. There are also those who strive to have more. We are all familiar with the phrase 'keeping up with the Joneses.' The need to demonstrate that you have what your neighbor has, can be either an internal or external perception of one's own worth. If I don't have what they have, I must strive for what they have, or be inferior.

Also, as I mentioned above from a positive perspective, how Friedrich Nietzsche described, "look at who you envy, and strive for what they have." Countless individuals have and continue to attempt to emulate Donald Trump, be it over the million people who bought his book *The Art of the Deal*, the cast members that played on *The Apprentice* who tried so hard to impress him, or the politicians that have tried to adopt his bravado style of skilled trash talk. These are all examples of those who envy, but who are also strong enough in their self identity to want to improve themselves. And perhaps an internal locus of control plays a factor in these situations.

Envy is one of the factors at the root of TDS. As we all know, envy typically has a darker side, one that is riddled with negative thoughts and actions. The negative side of envy is typically activated by those with a weak moral compass who are easily angered and susceptible to jealousy. Those who are consumed with envy usually have an external locus of control, poorly developed morals and ethics, and who are prone to groupthink. Such people become consumed with envy. There is an endless list of those who appear to be obsessed with Donald Trump and his accomplishments, and want to bring him down at any cost. Envy has contributed to the blind rage directed at him and has greatly contributed to the evolution of TDS.

Ask yourself how many times have you heard someone complaining about the former president regarding something trivial or making completely false accusations about him? That is TDS speaking. They simply can't admit to themselves that he has done great things for the country, and out of envy and spite, they would rather see the United States of America 'burn in hell' than give him credit.

After losing the presidential election in 2016, Hillary Clinton surely has exhibited extreme bouts of envy and continues to do so. She appears to be focused on her own perceived importance and seems to have lost touch with reality from my perspective, blaming just about anyone and as mentioned before conjuring up a litany of excuses as to how and why she was swindled out of becoming President 45. She has blamed Vladimir Putin, Barack Obama, James Comey, Mitch McConnell, Bernie Sanders, Jill Stein, Sexism, white resentment, a Democrat predecessor, Wikileaks, the media, political journalists, campaign financing, TV coverage, the debate questions, low information voters, and women under pressure from men. These are a few of the litany of excuses Hillary Clinton has made for crashing and burning in the 2016 election. She has even written a book titled *What Happened.* Unbelievable arrogance is rooted in what appears to be her own egocentrism and narcistic tendencies that present as second to none. I don't doubt for a minute that she sacrificed and did just about everything possible regardless of morality or ethics throughout her entire life striving to become the first female president. And, I suppose when one spends the entirety of their adult life, fifty years plus, pursuing such a lofty goal, one can occasionally become blind to any other potential outcome besides the one they feel they deserve.

In 2016 she started by blaming the FBI Director Jim Comey after he made a statement regarding her unsecured email server. For those of you who have forgotten, here is an excerpt from the FBI National Press

Office of his statement dated July 5, 2016:

> "Although we did not find clear evidence that Secretary
> Clinton or her colleagues intended to violate laws governing
> the handling of classified information, there is evidence
> that they were extremely careless in their handling of very
> sensitive, highly classified information. For example, seven
> e-mail chains concern matters that were classified at the Top
> Secret/Special Access Program level when they were sent
> and received. These chains involved Secretary Clinton both
> sending e-mails about those matters and receiving e-mails
> from others about the same matters. There is evidence to
> support a conclusion that any reasonable person in Secretary
> Clinton's position, or in the position of those government
> employees with whom she was corresponding about these
> matters, should have known that an unclassified system was no
> place for that conversation. In addition to this highly sensitive
> information, we also found information that was properly
> classified as Secret by the U.S. Intelligence Community at the
> time it was discussed on e-mail (that is, excluding the later
> "up-classified" e-mails). None of these e-mails should have
> been on any kind of unclassified system, but their presence
> is especially concerning because all of these e-mails were
> housed on unclassified personal servers not even supported
> by full-time security staff, like those found at Departments
> and Agencies of the U.S. Government—or even with a
> commercial service like Gmail. Separately, it is important to
> say something about the marking of classified information.
> Only a very small number of the e-mails containing classified

information bore markings indicating the presence of classified information. But even if information is not marked "classified" in an e-mail, participants who know or should know that the subject matter is classified are still obligated to protect it."

This statement by Jim Comey is not only an example of what Hillary Clinton was/is willing to do to obtain the highest position in the country, but it is also an example of her arrogant and narcissistic type behavior. What looks like Hillary's envy of her husband and of all the men who have held the office of president puts on display her misandrist attitude and has in my opinion, led her to flagrantly disregarding right from wrong. The experience has seemingly tested her moral judgment.

Speaking of Hillary makes me think of narcissism. Besides yearning to be admired, a narcissist has an excessive perception of their own importance. Other features of the narcissist include being entitled, arrogant, lacking in empathy; they are exploitative for gain and prefer associating with perceived important people. A narcissist is also preoccupied with success, power, and beauty. Is Hillary a narcissist? You be the judge … The diagnostic criteria include an extensive pattern of grandiosity. The DSM-5 stipulates that five or more criteria must be met. Well, in my opinion she is no slouch in this department, as she most likely meets five of the criteria before getting out of bed in the morning.

1. Has a grandiose sense of self-importance.
2. Is preoccupied with fantasies of unlimited success, power, brilliance, beauty, or ideal love.
3. Believes that she is "special" and unique and can only be understood by, or should associate with, other special or high-status people. Certainly not deplorables.

4. Requires excessive admiration.
5. Has a sense of entitlement.
6. Is interpersonally exploitative.
7. Lacks empathy.
8. Is often envious of others or believes that others are envious of her.
9. Shows arrogant, haughty behaviors or attitudes.

Envy and narcissism are inextricably tied together. Narcissists envy others, and at the same time believe others envy them. Furthermore, the narcissist will very often engage in destructive behavior toward others to fulfil their misguided needs and insure within their own mind that they are better than everyone else. This type of behavior is self-justified.

By September of 2022 and continuing through 2023, Hillary Clinton's description of conservatives has evolved on a negative trajectory from calling them "deplorables" to saying that Trump rally attendees were like Nazis, and that Donald Trump's speeches were like Adolf Hitler's. Perhaps it is simply egocentrism that makes her say things like that. What's that you ask? Egocentrism refers to a person's lack of ability to understand that other people can have a valid opinion or belief that differs from their own. A 2014 study by Steinbeis and Singer discussed how people will project their thoughts and emotions like envy or spite onto others, thereby indicating a degree of egocentrism.[67] They studied the neurocognitive mechanisms underlying emotional egocentricity, bias, and implemented a financially competitive game in their study that prompted feelings of envy and schadenfreude (getting pleasure from the misfortune of others). They found a correlation between envy and egocentric behavior with neural activity. Basically, it is a bias where someone assumes that other people share their view and can't imagine that other people's beliefs don't align with theirs. That certainly sounds just like Hillary and Barack's attitude as well as that of so many of their supporters.

I am reminded of Obama and his followers. He did a recent interview where he said something along the lines of, "There are people on the right who have a misconstrued sense of reality."[68] I find that he often tends to bloviate his beliefs, and implies that he can't imagine anyone truly thinking differently. That certainly sounds egocentric. I have met people that have exhibited similar traits. For example, when posed with a statement that not all people liked Barack Obama, they would scoff and say, "Don't be ridiculous; everyone liked him." Their ability to accept that someone had a belief system or thought that didn't directly coincide with theirs was simply preposterous and absolutely unthinkable. Talk about self absorbed and egotistical.

Another form of narcissism is referred to as collective narcissism. This happens when someone exhibits an exaggerated belief in the superiority of their in-group, be that a gang, religion, political orientation, or nation, etc., but deep down feels doubtful about their group's prestige and therefore craves its recognition by others. It was suggested that an in-group's perceived exceptionalism compensates for the individual's low self-esteem, therefore making the collective narcissist very defensive to threats of their group's views as it would directly impact their own self-esteem. The collective narcissist needs us to believe in their exceptionality; otherwise, they don't feel sufficiently appreciated. They are 'entitled' to be right, and 'need' others to agree with them; otherwise, they will look like the fools that we all see them as.[69]

As such, these people are likely very easily biased toward believing group ideology and conspiratorial thinking. A great example of this is the number of allegations that have been thrown at Donald Trump, and how so many on the left believe he should be locked up and not allowed to run for the office of president again. Their unrelenting attack on Donald Trump surely demonstrates the low self-esteem and shear panic of those attacking him. They will fight till their last breath to prove he is guilty of something—just anything in order to fulfill/justify all of the accusations they have made over the years. They will even retaliate to perceived attacks or provocations against the in-group, regardless of whether they are real, while at the same time potentially overlooking true threats. As well, collective narcissists have a tendency to be prejudiced, lack emotional regulation, with a propensity toward vindictiveness and hostility directed at those who dissent or are part of the out-group questioning the in-group's view. Consider that so many conservative blacks have been called out for supporting Donald Trump and the MAGA movement.

This inability of the in-group to accept any other view leads to hypersensitivity to insult. In other words, they have no tolerance for differing views. Evidence has shown that the collective, narcissistic in-group justifies its intergroup aggression as a defensive mechanism. The justification is explained in the form of provocation or undermining by the out-group, and since the in-group is 'morally superior,' it must therefore defend its views. Several studies have concluded that the collective narcissist tends to react with hostility, joyful malevolence or at a minimum, they enjoy another's suffering, even in situations that require some creative assumptions to be believed.[70]

Researchers from Nottingham Trent University found that liberals (aka Democrats) engaged in collective narcissism have a higher likelihood of believing fake news.[71] They attempted to understand why these reactions took place and studied a sample of 904 Americans with varying political views. When presented with two truthful stories about

President Trump, one positive and one negative, participants generally found the stories to be legitimate regardless of their political opinions; however, the study found that collective narcissism drove liberals' confidence toward putting more credence in the anti-Trump piece. The study reported that while conservatives displayed a degree of collective narcissism, the effect was not as statistically significant when considering the questions about Trump as it was with liberals. When presenting the results of their study at a British Psychological Society Conference, Dr. Harper said, "The concept of fake news has taken hold of political discourse since the election of President Trump in 2016, leading to the delegitimization of media outlets across the Western world on ideological or political grounds." He went on to say that, "Liberals believe news stories to maintain a favorable feeling about their own group. But Conservatives believe news stories because of a tendency to use their gut instincts." This demonstrated in my opinion how Democrats can be easily misled and manipulated when the narrative of a story fits what they want to believe, especially when they have the support of their peers.

Now, I know what you are thinking. Many people would describe Donald Trump as narcissistic, but a more accurate characterization describes him as being an *Alpha male*. There is a significant distinction between the narcissist and the Alpha male. The narcissist demonstrates a pattern of grandiosity, while the Alpha male has a proclivity to lift all those around him.

The Alpha male optimizes what TDS sufferers detest most—the man who is not afraid of being a man. Strong, decisive, willing to take the lead. One who is not afraid of speaking his mind, getting his hands dirty, helping others, or accepting criticism. He is powerful and always moving forward. The Alpha is usually the man who succeeds in life, and is admired by other men and desired by women. I could go on, but I think you get the picture. An Alpha male is comprised of many positive and admired attributes. However, in more recent times, it seems the Alpha has a nemesis in that of the new world feminists, the politically correct, and well ... the many that are jealous of the Alpha—the non-Alpha. The Alpha is becoming less prevalent in today's western world as he is being demonized by so many. The rise of the misandrist attitude is taking hold in our society to the significant detriment of young men. In today's world, there are those who despise the Alpha and want to stamp out masculinity from our society. You have likely heard some on the left describe the Alpha's behavior as 'Toxic Masculinity.' The negative labelling, I believe is born out of envy from those with low self-esteem. It is an attempt by the weak and ineffectual to eliminate those whom they secretly perceive as superior to them.

There are several designations of men, with Alpha being the Top Dog, so to say. Think Donald Trump. It does not mean that other men are less or not as good. It simply means they are different. That said, the Alpha male certainly has many of the positive attributes one would want in a leader, especially the president. This comes back to a common theme in this book, which speaks to being accountable for yourself. I discuss it when addressing millennials, political perspective, locus of control, sanctuary cities, etc. Are you seeing the theme? Those willing to step up, are perceived to be more of an Alpha. And those who try to appease are more of a Beta male. Sound familiar? The previous president went on what has been described as an apology tour (Beta Barack). Maybe I can take a page out of Donald Trump's book and create a new nickname for the previous president. Wonder what kind of man he is ... certainly not an Alpha!

Then there is Joe Biden. I say he falls under the Omega designation.

What do you think? I mean the designation of what an Omega is in the hierarchy of men. The Omega is one that can be described as the lowest in a hierarchal society, or can be referred to as the runt or lone wolf. Well, we know Joe Biden is not the latter. The Omega is one who is basically subordinate to all others in his group, and is expected to remain in that position. Hmmm, sounding familiar, maybe like the current resident of the White House? It certainly appears that Joe Biden has been pushed forward as an Omega figurehead, so to speak, with the likely expectation that he will be submissive to those within his circles. The perfect strawman. Its hard for me to even write about or accept that he is president considering all of the incompetency exhibited. I wonder who is pulling the strings, perhaps a previous candidate or president?

The 'have nots' always try to take away what the 'haves' have. In other words, they envy him, so they must take him down. This is a sort of support-for-the-underdog, take-down-the champ mentality. The Alpha is certainly on the endangered species list, and the left is pushing hard to make them extinct. But Donald Trump will have nothing to do with it!

The decline of the Alpha can be somewhat attributed to the millennial. "Why?" you ask. Well, if you accept the lazy, unmotivated, quitter stereotype of the millennial, it can lead one to assume that these underachievers have fewer friends, less education, less money, are out of shape and overweight, and are shedding testosterone by the pound. How many women do you know that are interested in meeting a low energy, unemployed, freeloading, couch-surfing gamer? Not too many, I suspect! Not a surprise considering twice as many men from that cohort are living with their parents when compared to women of the same age group. More and more women every year are getting higher education when compared to men. I suspect a resurgence of the Alpha is on the horizon because of President Trump. Most want to be an Alpha and typically tend to emulate the behaviors in order to improve their own standing in the hierarchy of their domain. The Alpha status is obtained through a variety of ways which can include physical prowess, financial success, social efforts, or building alliances within a group, to name a few.

Unlike the Alpha, the liberal narcissists detest any information source that goes against what they believe, and from my perspective, they implement this type of angry denial strategy in order to protect their fragile, bloated egos, and defend their low self-esteem. I realize it sounds a bit contradictory that someone can have both a bloated ego and low self-esteem, but think of the ego as a protecting factor or defence mechanism, and the bloated ego works as a type of shield that impowers them because they are "superior" in their minds. Another defense mechanism they incorporate is to avoid being near conservatives if by themselves or watching programs like *Fox News*, as the potential of information presented to them will challenge their pre-programmed psyche. They appear to be much more comfortable and even emboldened when with a group of like-minded liberals. Just think about how many times over the last few years the left wing mobs have shut down conservative speakers as they simply can't tolerate hearing a differing opinion. Sounds Marxist to me. They are empowered when in a group displaying collective narcissism and simply knowing that they are doing the "right thing." This way of thinking is so distorted, but they appear unable or unwilling to identify this as a problem, as it has been so deeply programmed into their mind by the socio-Marxist liberal progressive machine that they can't see anything else. I suspect these left wing narcissists truly believe in what they do and how they act as morally superior, or at a minimum, they want to be perceived as doing good. However, in an attempt to hold this higher position of moral clarity lies the contradiction of them repressing any negative effects of their behavior. They have found some internal way of accepting the belief that the end justifies the means. How can someone be morally superior when they won't allow others to share their thoughts and opinions?

Harper and Baguley studied the ideological asymmetries in perceptions of media legitimacy and determined that liberals are statistically more likely to use their righteousness of political views to accept politically-consistent news stories regardless of whether or not they are factual, and those who engaged in collective narcissism use their self perceived superiority, especially related to political views, which is demonstrated in their exaggerated legitimacy judgments to justify politically consistent anti-Trump stories.[72] In other words, their perceived superiority coupled with peer collective narcissism allows them to believe just about anything, especially if it fits the desired narrative regardless of whether it is 'Fake News.'

The growth and proliferation of TDS is rooted in the leftist mentality exacerbated by their external locus of control, weak moral development, their envious, narcissistic exhibitions, and misandrist attitudes naturally leading to irritational behavior justified by groupthink or mob mentality.

CHAPTER 7

GROUPTHINK

The Mob

"I don't believe in quotas. America was founded on
a philosophy of individual rights, not group rights.

- Clarence Thomas, Supreme Court Justice
1948-

I am sure most of you are familiar with the term 'groupthink,' but I would still like to provide a quick overview of how this sociological construct has led us to the currently tumultuous times.

The term was coined in the 1970s by Irving Janis, a research psychologist from Yale University.[73] He theorized that group pressures can lead to a collective failure of rational thought and decision-making, and to the degradation of mental efficiency and moral judgment in exchange for seeking alternatives that require critical thinking and decision-making.

Typically, groupthink is a byproduct of an in-group which is usually comprised of individuals who view things similarly, have shared identity, or interests, and find comfort in this familiarity. This comfort can lead to the individual not using their own skills of common sense and deductive reasoning, rooted in the effort to avoid upsetting the group. The phenomenon of groupthink occurs when a group of people reach an agreement or consensus without much or any critical thinking by the individual. It is also more likely to occur when individuals belonging to an in-group have more cohesiveness within the group, which is insulated from outside sources of information. The groupthink mentality of a cohesive group leads to thinking that they are superior. They tend to think of out-group members as outsiders who are dumb, evil, or just generally inferior. These beliefs allow the in-group to justify any acts of violence or inhumanity toward their opponents, and in a sense to justify the means to an end. Think about the Salem witch trials of the seventeenth century. They are evidence of extreme groupthink leading to mass hysteria and culminating from the consequences of religious extremism, false allegations, and ultimate mis-steps in the legal processes.[74] Or think of the Challenger disaster ... a flawed decision process due to groupthink. Think Democrats that only watch CNN.... One group, with one news source.

Those who are less happy, have lower self-esteem, and have an external locus of control are in my opinion much more likely to be susceptible to groupthink. The attributes I just mentioned appear to be more prevalent in those on the left, so it is easy to reason that they are more malleable in their thinking and therefore a target population for recruitment into the left wing ideological army. Let's face it. We all like being part of a group. Remember the old television sitcom series *Cheers*? You have to sing the following lines:

> "Sometimes you want to go
> Where everybody knows your name
> And they're always glad you came."

Whatever it may be, it usually feels good to belong, which would be considered an aspect of being part of the 'in-group' that may lead to 'groupthink.'

Groupthink (also described as 'hive thinking' by some) can go in a very negative direction even though a consensus may be reached, utilizing those with low self-esteem to develop a mutual agreement that may be derived under faulty and uniformed decision-making. Additionally, this way of thinking usually precludes listening to dissenting opinions and the denial of potential negative outcomes. It evolves when an individual tends to follow group decision-making rather than using their own judgment. It can stem from a person's reluctance or inability to make their own decisions, or it can be because belonging gives them false confidence, believing that they are invulnerable and are morally superior because they have the support and consensus of 'everyone.' While each person has their own mind, they work together almost without thought to accomplish a goal that has been established by a single member or a few members of their group similar to what you would find in a bee hive or ant colony.

Conformity of the group can quickly lead to dysfunction and irrational behavior regardless of how well-intentioned they are. The conformity sometimes generates and perpetuates ignorance, pushing individuals to act in a way that they typically wouldn't. For example, from my understanding, historically, reporters would go into the field, interview people, do research, collect evidence, verify, and corroborate their information from a variety of sources, and then present a story. But, in today's environment, it appears that this is no longer the norm in a number of cases. The hypothesis of 'media bubbles' has led to extreme ignorance when gathering and disseminating news. "What is a media bubble?" you ask? Author, Eli Pariser initially described this trend as a 'Filter Bubble' in his best-selling book of the same name, which in his words describes how "internet users get less exposure to conflicting viewpoints and are isolated intellectually in their own 'informational bubble.'[75] Nate Silver, an American statistician, pointed out that the ideological clustering in top newsrooms leads to 'groupthink.'[76] Basically, he infers that most reporters have succumbed to what he calls a 'media bubble.' That is when most in the media, talk, and tweet with others in their circle of contemporaries/colleagues that have their same beliefs, especially those within the DC Beltway when referring to political news, and in which that is their primary source for obtaining information. In other words, they were not looking for conflicting views whatsoever; they were happy obtaining confirmation of their already preconceived notions—more of an affirmation to move ahead, than a deep dive into independent research. In reality, group-think is the opposite of the scientific approach.

Journalism Professors Nikki Usher and Yee Man Margaret Ng from the University of Illinois conducted a study of how Washington-based journalists interact and learn from one another through what appears to be extensive research and analysis.[77] They determined that the journalists in the Beltway region formed nine clusters. These nine clusters were made up of microbubbles of smaller proportions than they had initially thought the journalists were operating within. These smaller, more condensed bubbles suggested that there should be even more concern regarding groupthink and insular thinking coming from the Beltway journalists.

When reflecting on politics in 2016, the ignorance grew exponentially through groupthink to the point where it seemed that no reporters could fathom the idea of Donald Trump winning the election. Then low and behold as the evening progressed on November 8, 2016, the 'shock and awe' began to set in. It put on display the media's ignorance and showed how out of touch they were with the American people. Donald Trump was not going to let them get away with it either. He had been calling them out for months, and this was confirmation of what he had been telling his supporters from the beginning. Not surprisingly though, there had been a distaste for Donald Trump and the Republican Party by the media as it is grossly overrepresented by Democrats. As of 2013, it was cited that only 7 percent of journalists were Republicans, and that the media is basically infested with Democrats.[78] The ignorance created through this groupthink media bubble has only escalated since the 2016 election as no one *was*, or *is* willing to accept any wrongdoing, as they keep pushing their left wing ideology. A study from Syracuse University found a further decrease in Republican representation of journalists, down to 3.4 percent in 2022.[79] With each month passing since Donald Trump's inauguration, tensions between him and the media appeared to escalate, and continued even beyond his presidency. In my opinion, they were simply embarrassed because of their own incompetence and likely haven't felt much relief since Donald Trump left office as he remains front and center on the political stage. Donald Trump won't cave in. He is a scrapper. Even well after he left the office of the president, you can see the unjustified negative behavior of the media continuing.

The media along with numerous left wing groups are doing whatever they can to discredit Donald Trump and splinter the Republican Party by calling Trump supporters extremists, fanatical, and any kind of "ism" that suits the day. For example, two shootings occurred in August of 2019 that generated a considerable amount of rhetoric and protest.[80] Somehow a link between these actions and Donald Trump was being made? During the same timeframe, Donald Trump had made statements indicating his disgust and denouncement of any and all hate and discrimination. The *New York Times* attempted to report this fact and proclaimed, "Trump Urges Unity Vs. Racism" as their headline after President Trump denounced bigotry and racism once again.[81] The left rallied against the *New York Times*, successfully bullying the newspaper to change their headline. Not only did numerous readers threaten to cancel their subscriptions, but several outspoken politicians—some of whom were 2020 hopefuls—quickly tweeted against the headline. Cory Booker, Kirsten Gillibrand, Beto O'Rourke, and Bill de Blasio, to name a few, tweeted about how offensive or even racist this headline was. A wave of criticism was so fast and furious that the *New York Times* changed the headline for all subsequent editions.[82] Trump Derangement Syndrome strikes once again. This form of overt censoring/bullying propagated by way of groupthink is an attempt to alter American ideology and shift it farther to the left. The truth needs to be reported, and organizations as well as individuals need to grow a spine and simply stop being bullied by the left wing extremists.

The media calls him a fascist and an authoritarian, and *Times Magazine* even ran an opinion piece discussing how similar Donald Trump is to Hitler among a litany of other derogatory labels, when actually the current administration under Biden is turning the country into a police state with their underlying support—or at least unwillingness to discredit—Antifa and BLM.[83] Left leaning forces arrested Trump supporters, served search warrants, seized property, and went beyond what a normal, Democratic society would expect, but at the same time ignoring the left wing radicals' transgressions. The more people on the left, driven by popular media and culture, are spoon-fed how horrible Trump supporters are, the more they accept and believe it. I think political analyst Steve Bannon said it well. "It's just a circle of people talking to themselves who have no fucking idea what's going on."[84] The US does not consist wholly of densely populated coastal cities, and once the media comes to that realization, there would likely be more equal coverage of ideas which would help bring the country together. This actually, is not strictly an example of groupthink, as it also taps into gaslighting, which is something I will discuss in an upcoming chapter.

Another example of groupthink ... The general population in New York and the immediate tri-state area hate Donald Trump. The irony of most people's distain for Donald Trump is that he is a classic New Yorker. This distain is especially true of people living in New York and surrounding areas. He is an incredibly successful New Yorker; he exhibits the typical personality characteristics of so many people I have met from New York. It is almost humorous that such a large portion of Democrats are from New York, the home of Donald Trump, as they have such similar personalities. If you have ever travelled to New York, you will understand exactly what I mean. Nearly every person I have met from New York is wonderful. That said, in general they tend to be a little louder and bolder than say someone from Iowa or Indiana. While some may see those as negative attributes, I simply believe them to be only a few of the interesting and fun characteristics of people from that region. Donald Trump is simply behaving like a typical New Yorker, but the legacy networks and social media platforms telegraph their disdain for Trump, so New Yorkers buy into the propaganda, falling into lock step with left wing ideology.

Groupthink can also lead to dangerous behaviors. The left's ideology and methodology can be described as aligning with the classic terrorist in that they use psychological and social principals of behavioral, emotional, and group dynamics to influence individuals and populations for political purposes. And when all else fails, a shift toward violence is deemed acceptable. Ultimately, the goal of a terrorist as we know them in a traditional sense, is someone who uses violence to create the natural fear of death or mutilation to control thought, speech, and to shape political behavior in order to replace it with their construct of what *should* be. These political 'terrorists' are well versed in using psychological warfare by implementing the use of fear, violence, or the threats thereof at the most primal levels in order to elicit a reaction, to shape behavior, and to advance their agenda. Maxine Waters, Eric Holder "Crazy Nancy", " Cory Booker, "Crooked" Hillary Clinton, etc. have all made some sort of direct or veiled threat of violence. There has been no shortage of that from the left Calls to, "Get in people's faces," and "Kick them (Republicans) when they go low," and "You cannot be civil," and to "Harass cabinet officials" and " You have to be ready to throw a punch."[85] The desired outcome is typically control—to the detriment or destruction of the current political system. These comments may seem innocuous on the surface, but make no mistake, when in the right environment, they can become the precursor to aggressive and yes, sometimes violent or deadly behavior. You don't have to look very far to find evidence of the like. Steve Scalise was severely injured, and numerous other Republicans were shot at on June 14, 2017, when they were holding a practice session for the Congressional Baseball Game for Charity by left wing nut job James Hodgkinson. U.S. Capitol Police Officer Crystal Griner, congressional aide Zack Barth, and lobbyist Matt Mika were also shot by the left wing shooter. The Virginia Attorney General concluded the shooter's attack was, "an act of terrorism ... fueled by rage against Republican legislators."[86]

Who is more violent? The left or the right? Well, while doing research for this book, I came across a number of Democrats who espouse that all Republicans are violent, which is simply untrue (gaslighting), and that when a Democrat happens to be violent, it is considered an isolated incident and the behavior should not be generalized across all

Democrats. I find it very interesting that the common-sense belief of not generalizing can be applied to one side of the political aisle, but not the other. Then I thought maybe it had to do with Republicans' tendency to support the Second Amendment and subsequent likelihood of owning a gun. This confusion, purposeful or not is simply not justifiable. Simply owning a gun does not make someone violent. It is rather a safety precaution to protect themselves from someone who is violent.

Antifa is a colorful example of groupthink. Cambridge dictionary defines Antifa as "groups of people who oppose fascism and who show this using protests and sometimes violence."[87] This organization of dysfunctional losers has perpetrated numerous transgressions against a wide swath of the public. In a number of cities, the civic politicians have asked their local police to stand down and to allow Antifa to exercise their 1st Amendment rights, while at the same time smashing windows and beating up people that don't agree with their ridiculous philosophy. Antifa is comprised of those susceptible to groupthink as a majority of them are likely still living in their 'momma's basement' as President Trump likes to say. And they generally struggle with making their own decisions about leading a productive lifestyle.

The reaction to Antifa's actions is in direct contrast to how the people of the January 6th rally on the capitol were designated and subsequently treated. I think they (the left) have ignored the components of the First Amendment regarding the right to *peaceably* assembly and that of *free speech*. For example, Andy Ngo is a Portland Oregon-based conservative reporter who was covering the militant group Antifa and who was subsequently attacked on June 29, 2019 and beaten and humiliated by their members during one of their many so-called peaceful demonstrations.[88] The left wing media, albeit mostly insignificant players, have attempted to justify that behavior by stating the Mr. Ngo

TRUMP DERANGEMENT SYNDROME

had 'doxxed' some Antifa members. Again, this behavior suits the left, but not the right.

Can you imagine if Trump supporters went out and beat the people who 'doxxed' the right-leaning Supreme Court Justices in the summer of 2022 when the decision to overturn Roe v. Wade came down. There were protests and threats to murder some of these justices, and this behavior was even condoned by the current so-called president. Additionally, protesters were threatening to burn down the country simply because they didn't get their way. This is a clear example of groupthink justification. This is also a great example of TDS at the highest level with perpetrators on the left destroying communities, setting buildings on fire, and violently hurting people with limited or no reaction from the government. However, those on the right that were peacefully walking through the US Capitol building on January 6th, were designated as terrorists with a good number of them being put in jail. One gentlemen Matt Perna who attended the January 6th Stop the Steal rally was facing BS charges that could have landed him in prison for nine years. After dealing with several delays of his trial, the potential sentence he was faced with, and combined with the attacks on his character that demoralized him, Mr. Perna very sadly took his own life. His family remarked that, "His community, which he loved, his country and the justice system killed his spirit and his zest for life."[89]

While this man has taken his life for what I believe to be unjust persecution, there were riots over the next few years associated with so-called anti-fascist groups that were roaming the streets of America uncontrolled, bullying and beating into submission anyone who disagreed with them without repercussions.

This is simply another gross exaggeration of the situation where the establishment decided to flex its political muscle to ensure compliance of anyone who might even think about opposing them. People were locked away without being charged, tracked down from phone and credit card records to be interrogated, and charged—over 1,100 people. Some who were in DC on that day were sentenced to over twenty-two years in prison. The message from the left was, "Don't Mess With Us."

It's just like the Canadian truckers rally where the ridiculous Justin Trudeau (elected with only 33 percent of votes) froze people's bank accounts (were debanked), took away their vehicle insurance, and locked away some people all because he was too afraid to simply come out and speak to the people showing concern for individual rights.[90] Talk about flexing political muscle to take away freedom of speech. And yet they have so many fooled…. These leaders act like they are doing these things for the good of the country, whereas it is truly about their own ego and power as they are acting like Marxist dictators.

According to the left wing mentality, it is acceptable to revert to violence to stop Trump and his supporters. These exhibitions of rioting and destruction is mob mentality on steroids. All the while, the left wing media turns a blind eye, which shows how pervasive TDS has become. It rises from the street-level animals to the newsrooms of America and beyond, displaying how the syndrome has become saturated through all levels of society on the left. Even the liberal mayor of Portland Ted Wheeler has boarded the train to insanity. On several occasions, he has said he likes to use a hands-off approach, and he has told the Portland Police to 'stand down' when Antifa is gathering.[91] I think he means to say protesting and inciting violence is just fine! This approach includes Antifa's intimidation, rioting, use of violence (as in Portland October 2018), diverting traffic, and basically taking over territory, which has gone unchecked in many cities around the country.

In 2019 Antifa members are witnessed calling police officers "pigs" and throwing rocks at these same police.[92] Now I can't focus all of the blame on Mr. Wheeler, even though he is the leader of that community because groupthink has infiltrated grass roots movements all the way up to the White House. Included are Mr. Wheeler, along with several of his counterparts on the West Coast like former Oakland Mayor Libby Schaaf, who purposefully warned illegal immigrants that ICE raids were going to be conducted, and San Francisco's Mayor London Breed who put out a list of all cities across the USA where immigration raids were to be held, calling them "unconscionable."[93] This is just a short list of left-wing politicians who are displaying some of the symptoms of TDS by falling into groupthink behavior and making irrational decisions without considering what is best for their constituents as well as all American citizens.

Through a trickle down approach, if the president and governors feel a particular way, then one can only assume that civic politicians will possibly have the same belief system if they belong to the same political party. Their distaste for police services, the rule of law, and the American way of life is somewhat understandable because of their association with the Democrat Party and previous leadership. Barack Obama and his wife on many occasions inferred that racism is still very prevalent in the USA and that the police are racist. I specifically recall him commenting on an unfortunate situation on July 7, 2016, when a police officer shot someone during a traffic stop. Philando Castile a thirty-two-year-old Black American was pulled over for a broken tail light in Minnesota by twenty-eight-year-old Latino officer Jeronimo Yanez and was subsequently shot.

Governor Mark Dayton of Minnesota stated," Philando Castile would be alive if he were white."[94] You have several West Coast politicians, the current governor of Minnesota, and *the President of The*

United States at the time indicating that there is a serious problem with police as a whole, and that racism is a major contributor.[95] Am I missing something? Constable Yanez is Latino, *not White*! I truly believe this to be an awful situation, but I feel that Barack Obama took advantage of the situation to continue promoting negativity towards police agencies as well as racism between whites and blacks. I recall being stunned when he made those comments. If you examine the negative belief system from the leader of the country as it descends to the state and city levels, it only makes sense that it will naturally influence the general population creating and reinforcing dissention. Antifa and BLM become mainstream …

However, what happens when the tendency to maintain unity in a group (groupthink) is so high that you're not allowed to have different opinions? What happens when no one dares to disagree? A plague descends on your country, which is exactly what is happening in many places across America today. I have seen groups try to take over restaurants and forcibly make people agree with them. For example; telling people to raise their hands in solidarity with the BLM movement, and if they refused, the intimidation is amplified. I am sure that would be most unsettling for the majority of people, especially considering the extreme cases of violence that have been initiated by these groups on an increasingly regular basis. Another incident of aggressive behavior was perpetrated in Wilmington, Delaware in August of 2020. Yes, the home of Joe Biden.

This is amazing; two young women (Olivia Winslow and Camryn Amy) approached a seven-year-old boy as he was taking a stand and expressing his political views with some home-made signs and a MAGA hat. I can tell you already know where this is going … They tore up his signs and stole his hat. The incident was caught on video by the young man's mother.[96] As you would suspect, things escalated, and started to become somewhat physical. The mother rightfully encouraged her son to stand up for himself, and asked for the hat to be returned. He was not hurt physically, although I suspect the event will have long-lasting ramifications emotionally. Hopefully, this experience will eventually unfold in a positive way that leads him in the future to become a Republican politician who continues to stand up to bullies like those two. Thankfully, the two losers were arrested and charged with robbery, conspiracy, and endangering the welfare of a child. One last point on this incident. Since it happened in the town where Joe Biden lives, and he has been and wants to continue being a representative of the people, where in the hell was he in defending this young man's right to free speech? He was seven years old! Joe Biden should have denounced the aggressor's behavior. This incident demonstrates how irrational people can become when inflicted with TDS.

These actions are happening across the country and unfolding in various ways, but all have the same goal: to intimidate and silence the Right. A perfect example of this unfolded before my eyes, and I suspect it is very similar to what a number of you have experienced. I was recently out with some friends for dinner, and of course the topic of politics found its way to the table. It was disclosed that someone was a moderate Republican and that they liked to proudly wear MAGA clothing except for the fact that her husband suggested otherwise out of fear of her being shot. Additionally, her husband disclosed that he actually registered as a Democrat in order to stop being audited by the federal government. He experienced two audits as a Republican; zero audits as a Democrat … interesting I would say.

Back to my point regarding left wing violence and intimidation, and how their groupthink can shape others' behavior. Not being able to say or express what we think out of fear of retribution is at the root of fascism. The scary fact is that these fears are justified when you see the aggressive insanity perpetrated by people like Shannon Brandt, the Democrat left wing nut job that ran down and killed Cayler Ellingson, a young man in North Dakota in 2022 because as he proclaimed, "he was a MAGA supporter" and that "made him [Brandt] afraid."[97] As a footnote, Brandt only received a sentence of five years with part of that being served at home. Ridiculous!

As you can see from the examples above, groupthink has pushed the negative narrative of the left, framing the characterizations of Donald Trump and Republicans as immoral, sexist, homophobic, violent, dysfunctional dregs on society. PC culture, and wokeism has been weaponized and utilized by the left in group action to force those that disagree to conform. In essence they are gaslighting.

GASLIGHTING

The Art of Deception

"You can fool all the people some of the time
and some of the people all the time, but you
cannot fool all the people all the time."

- Abraham Lincoln, President of the United States
1809-1865

Gaslighting is a term that made its first appearance in the English language in the early twentieth century, but then faded away somewhat until more recently with a resurgence in the media. Gaslighting is a form of persistent psychological bullying, manipulation, and brainwashing that is intended to cause the victim to doubt him or herself, and to ultimately lose their own sense of perception, identity, and self-worth. The statements and accusations made by the perpetrator are often based on mistruths and marginalization. The purpose is to undermine their target's confidence in their own ability to decern right from wrong or reality from fiction, subsequently leaving the victim dependent on the perpetrator for their thoughts and feelings.

Gaslighting is grounded in manipulating another's sense of reality, and is a type of mental trickery. It can be in the form of someone or an entity trying to convince someone else that they are guilty of something or that something did or did not happen; however, it is actually the initiator who is typically guilty of doing or suggesting the action in question. Maybe a better way of explaining it is to think of it as someone manipulating the reality of someone else. Politicians can, and do use gaslighting strategies, and they regularly operate via the exploitation of social vulnerabilities. Now, if you do a little research, you will see that gaslighting primarily pertains to the individual, which I suppose makes sense, as the term was brought into the mainstream by a great, old 1944 Ingrid Bergman psychological thriller of the same name: *Gaslight.* A woman's husband is slowly and systematically manipulating her into believing she is going insane.

The manipulation of others takes many forms. For example, someone might make up stories and tell someone they are being watched. In fact, the person making up the stories is the watcher. The surveillance, subsequently leads to the victim questioning and feeling that they are being watched.

Or on a broader sense, one can tell a society that the reason something is happening is one person's or a political party's fault. Accusers assign unjustified blame to one person or a political party. It is said that if you keep hearing the same thing enough times, you will begin to believe it to be true, regardless of whether it has any merit or whether it is grounded in reality.

Gaslighting can describe classic Democrat liberal behavior. A recent example is when Joe Biden started to declare that it was Donald Trump's fault that a number of college and professional sports were not being played during the spring and summer of 2020, while in reality, it was the organizations choice to stop playing as a result of the coronavirus.[98] Ultimately it was not President Trump's fault that the world was infected by the Chinese virus.

Unless of course, you believe that the release of the virus was a retaliation by the Chinese because of all the tariffs President Trump placed on them in the preceding year. Hmmm, that's food for thought ... However, back to my original point: It is much more likely that Joe Biden and his supporters kept beating that drum in an attempt to pull votes away from Donald Trump in November. The fact is that Donald Trump was advocating strongly for athletes to get back to what they do best. That approach would be good for the economy and the mental health of both spectators and participants.

Or how about the Democrats on many occasions stating that Donald Trump would have to be physically removed from the White House if and when he lost the election. Even Joe Biden said that, "I am absolutely convinced they will escort him from the White House with great dispatch" as he will likely refuse to leave on his own accord.[99] He also alleged that Donald Trump would try to steal the election stating, "This president is going to try and steal this election. This is a guy who said all mail-in ballots are fraudulent."[100] Remember what I said above about gaslighting? This is classic liberal gaslighting and projection. They blame others for what they are actually doing, in an attempt to misdirect and manipulate everyone's thinking. These statements come from a guy who stated that, "I absolutely" agree that Donald Trump is an "illegitimate president."[101] Classic gaslighting! We all know that Donald Trump is a staunch patriot who has nothing but respect for the office of the president, the White House, and all of the tradition and ceremony associated with the position. He simply exudes pride, and experiences enjoyment in the formality of the long-established customs and traditions that come along with being elected the President of the United States.

Gaslighters and narcissists are similar in that both tend to lie and exaggerate with a focus on presenting themselves with high regard while demeaning others. The narcissist typically attempts to come off as superior or special by exhibiting braggadocio. The narcissist shows off, or claims credit for an accomplishment they had nothing to do with in order to elevate their own self-worth. On the other hand, gaslighters are somewhat more aggressive in that they use psychological intimidation to make their target feel inferior and to establish control over their prey by utilizing constant criticism and false accusations. Both the gaslighter and the narcissist are usually skilled at distorting facts and fabricating falsehoods, as well as being experts at coercion. In the mind of a gaslighter, aggressiveness is the best defence when dealing with people. It is how the left frequently calls Donald Trump and those on the right racist, misogynist, xenophobic, extremists, etc....

Many narcissists and gaslighters enjoy 'getting away' with violating societal rules and norms. For example, narcissists tend to cut in line, invade others' personal space, sabotage others' achievements, or use other people's things without permission or without returning them. They also tend to under tip, break traffic laws, and won't arrive at appointments or keep promises.

Gaslighters tend to make marginalizing remarks, attempt to shame and humiliate others, use sardonic or sarcastic comments and angry or hateful speech, and they virulently attack those they deem undesirable.

Another large-scale example of gaslighting being perpetrated by the left is in regard to racism. I can hear the "Ooos" and "Ahhhs.".... Relax. I am not saying racism doesn't exist, as it surely does around the globe in many forms, but I don't believe it to be nearly as prevalent in America as the left would lead us to believe. By no means am I an expert in this area, but I have observed behavior throughout my lifetime, watched footage of riots and heinous activities, and read numerous history books about the subject. So, I feel that I have as much knowledge on the subject as the average individual. Nowadays, the left interjects various key words from their standard gaslighting playbook when attempting to crush their opponents. Racism is certainly at the top of their list along with the words xenophobic, sexist, homophobic, and systemic ... when trying to make the opposition look evil. This constant barrage of keywords is incorporated into their everyday language in order to sow tension between races, genders, and political ideologies, etc. And the sad thing is that it works! These key words are great dividers. Especially in today's world, where the 24-hour media is left-leaning and always needs a story ripe for the picking. I suspect this behavior is frustrating to all of the rational, upstanding people in the country regardless of their background.

No getting upset if I don't include you here, but I can just imagine how many white people are frustrated, saddened, disappointed, and disgusted when a white police officer hurts (or worse) a person of color, as when Rodney King was brutally beaten in Los Angeles in the 1990s. That was truly despicable! And, I believe that many black people are equally frustrated, saddened, disappointed, and disgusted when they see a group of black people smashing windows, looting, and attacking people during what were supposed to be peaceful protests. These are examples of what I suspect to be the bad apples from each race and certainly not the majority by any means. But the way the media portrays these incidents makes everyone look bad, and it propagates stereotypes, hatred, racism, and division in such a way as to be almost self prophecy. Like I said. "Say it enough, and people will start to believe it to be true." But ... the motivated, inquisitive person can dig deeper, and question what has been spoon-fed to them to decide for themselves what is the probable truth. The left has now created an environment where people of different races or backgrounds—particularly the younger generation—are uncomfortable discussing these issues with each other.

Let's look at all of the fraudulent activity that took place, or was denied to have taken place during and soon after the 2020 election. You be the judge.[102] Look at the excuses, and how things are written and slanted in particular ways to drive a narrative. Often, the narrative seems to be written with an agenda rather than to simply tell the facts. Those agendas repeatedly seem to find a way of covering for or excusing liberal behavior while condemning Donald Trump and conservative actions and labeling his supporters as "MAGA Extremists." I suspect that no one had the courage to come forward and take a stand regarding the 2020 election, as this would have been a significant black mark on the US, particularly on the global stage. So many statements have been made with conviction that no fraud or cheating took place in the 2020 election. Then how is it that within the following years some local elections have been questioned or overturned for exactly the same reasons that were claimed, but denied in 2020.

Government employee Wanda Geter was caught on video surveillance in 2023 purportedly stuffing ballot boxes with absentee ballots for a local election.[103] Fortunately, the people of Connecticut have a commonsense judge that saw the video and realized that the election more than likely was not conducted in a legal and fair manner, so he overturned the results and called for another election to be conducted. This same sort of evidence has been captured on numerous cameras from the 2020 presidential election, but nothing was done about it. Rather, anyone who contested that election was deemed a "conspiracy theorist" or "wacko" or "MAGA extremist." The media strongly agreed with the claims that it was a fair and legal election, and gaslit the majority of the American public, even going as far as to pursue and arrest people who voiced their disagreement, like those from January 6th who peacefully protested. The entire January 6th event has been blown out of proportion by the left and by Nancy Pelosi's followers redirecting everyone's attention away from the true cause for the protest. This march was extremely threatening to the left because their agenda and the power of the people was on full display. They were unable to hide the sheer number of people—in the hundreds of thousands, more likely surpassing a million attended—but the media have claimed that less than 50,000 people attended and that they were protesting the election results and supporting Trump. So, detractors schemed to change the narrative to focus on an issue that was even greater than election integrity … insurrection! The Million Maga March on November 14, 2020, just several weeks earlier, gave the liberals a preview of the magnitude of the people's support for Donald Trump.

The Million Maga March on November 14, 2022. Wow! What an experience! The positive energy, respect, and pride to be an American on that day was overwhelming to say the least. People from all corners of the country came out to support their president and their fellow American. The flags, banners, hats, T-shirts supporting Donald Trump went as far as the eye could see. The right and ability to assemble in the nation's capitol couldn't have been more important on that day, for the attendees after what appeared to be a very questionable election. What was perceived as a miscarriage of justice in a stolen election was at the forefront of everyone's mind, and by the millions, they marched on Washington as the constitution grants them the right to do so. While marching down Pennsylvania Avenue, then Constitution, to First Street like a powerful overflowing river in what was certainly the largest gathering of people I had ever been a part of, or even witnessed on television. You could see the confluence of throngs of supporters merging in from Louisiana Avenue then Delaware Avenue to join what seemed an unstoppable force of patriotism calling the election results into question. True Americans arrived on the footstep of the Supreme Court to let the Justices know that something had obviously gone awry with the 2020 election, and that they were not going to stand for it. It was quite a spectacle, not only to see the diverse group of people packed into the area around the courthouse, but to see how it filled almost ever nook and cranny of every road in the region.

As we stood and watched, prideful exuberance filled the air; there were chants supporting Donald Trump and various notable public speakers helping show their support from a small platform in front of the courthouse. All the time, you would see people functioning as emissaries, working their way through the crowd up-and down-stream to report on what was happening along the route. While doing this they maintained a communal sense of esprit de corp.

We met a young man and his girlfriend from Nashville I believe, who sat next to me to rest his sore feet because he wore his work boots to the march out of principal. He was in DC working for the President on that day! He stated that he needed to move $200 around to make it work, but this was so important that he did it. And he said he would be meeting me back in DC if the president needed us again. The East Indian women and her friends, who came from Baltimore, described being shamed in their hometown by numerous leftists in the community including at work, bullying her to the point that she couldn't speak about conservative ideals. Two young guys from out in the country near Winston-Salem and their dog that made the trip on what looked like their last dollar. They seemed somewhat uncomfortable in the city, but said they needed to be there. As I petted their dog, they shared thoughts with others nearby from California and Texas. The young man with the T-shirts saying, "token black kid" let me take a picture with him, mocking liberals' perspective on conservative people of color. Just to note, there were tons of black people at the march supporting Donald Trump. The women I met outside of the Trump hotel were apparently feeling very emotional and near tears as they watched the supporters heading toward freedom plaza to assemble. I can't say my emotions were much different. There was a group of guys, presumably Greeks from NY because of the accents. I heard them behind me on the march as we crested the hill next to the capitol building. When we saw another wall of Trump supporters streaming toward us from a different direction, they commented that it reminded them of a scene from Game of Thrones—like multiple armies coming together to fight a common enemy. The nice lady in the powered scooter who sat, watched, and took it all in … her husband and son with his Buck knife by his side often headed through the crowd to explore, listen, and observe, and then came back to share stories from the field. Some ladies pointed out the *Say Yes to the Dress* guy to my wife. He was so friendly and generous with his time. There was the guy wearing the LOTSA-Gays-Back-Trump T-shirt and the man carrying the enormous US Marine Corp Flag. He looked so tired by the time he got to the Supreme Court, but he held on strong and proud. I met individuals from just about every state in the union—young and old, men and women, gay and straight, rich and poor, of all colors and backgrounds; thank goodness we all showed up in DC to have the back of a president who has had our back for four years. It was a pleasure walking with you all, and it gave me a little extra pride to be an American. Thanks to all of the people who said, "Enough BS," got in their vehicles, bought plane tickets, thumbed a ride, or found some other way of making it to the capitol and banded together as one. Yes, one group was made up of black, brown, red, yellow, and white. All brothers and sisters were standing up to the divisive left in order to let them know we won't take it anymore. Donald Trump may be the tip of the spear, but We the People are the force behind it, thrusting it into the heart of those who hate our way of life. United we stand, my brothers!

Oh yeah, one last thing … a big thank you to the police of Washington DC for keeping us safe!

January 6th is a very similar situation in that overall, it was generally peaceful, positive, and patriotic. When you take into consideration the number of people who were in attendance versus those who were actually involved in destructive behavior, it would likely be much less than 1 percent of attendees. Now, I wasn't there on J6, but I certainly believe some external forces were thrown into the mix to make things go as they did. Unsuccessfully, I might add. There were a few skirmishes, a few broken windows, and oh wait … an unarmed protester by the name of Ashli Babbitt (a 12-year US Airforce veteran) who was shot and killed by the Capitol Police. But the way the media tends to write this up, it sounded more like an attempted overthrow of the US government. What BS! If you do a Google search, you will see headlines like, "Armed mob of supporters of the outgoing president," or "At least seven people dead," or "Supporters of Trump raid the Capitol." I am sure that there are enough intelligent, trained, and capable individuals out there that if they wanted to 'overthrow' the government, they would have done one hell of a better job than what unfolded on J6. The narrative was obviously orchestrated by the left to make the right look bad. Even the Chief of the Capitol Police agrees.[104] As far as the other people who unfortunately passed away during that period, they passed either from natural causes, accidental overdose, or suicide in the following days or weeks, not on J6. However, in today's age

CHAPTER 8 : GASLIGHTING

of over-the-top slanderous and sensational media coverage, anything associated with the 45th President of the United States is painted with a negative brush or hidden away from public consumption. The only thing the media wanted that day was to promote how awful a person Donald Trump was and that he was inciting his 'cult-like' supporters to destroy the capitol and overthrow the government. It was a left-wing feeding frenzy, where they were all piling on in a tragically gleeful celebration of the supposed downfall of their nemesis. A rally was portrayed as an insurrection.

The slight-of-hand that was perpetrated by Nancy Pelosi and her army of cronies during that timeframe was executed perfectly and has led to everyone still talking about her smoke screen as if it were the important event of that day. *Insurrection*! Batten down the hatches! The deplorables are coming! They are going to overthrow the government and kill us all! The total misdirection and BS on January 6th has successfully directed the attention away from why people travelled to march on DC that day in the first place. Pelosi had razor wire fences installed around the U.S. Capitol the next day and the National Guard was stationed for the following five months (all presumably for optics), with the mayor ordering a curfew—all after the march was over.

Meanwhile the summer before, people were destroying cities across America including DC, and they were described as 'peaceful' even though you could see flames and destruction in the background during newscasts. I'm getting away from the point I was trying to make regarding J6. The clear majority of hundreds of thousands if not millions of people travelled to DC from around the country and beyond to show their patriotic support of the country and to voice their opinion that the 2020 election wasn't void of corruption and deceit, and to support election integrity during the Stop the Steal Rally. The president asked everyone there more than once during his speech to march peacefully and patriotically to the capitol to share their thoughts, which the majority did.

Another example of large scale gaslighting is in regard to the federal election bellwether indicators we have been told to ignore by the media regarding the 2020 election. A bellwether is a leader or an indicator of trends and can definitely be applied in this arena as it pertains to the 2020 election. Trump won 18 of 19 bellwether counties throughout the country.[105] Most of them had chosen the correct winner for the office of the president for over fifty years, and some were correct as far back as the late 1940s. These bellwether regions are looked at as microcosms of larger areas or populations that are synonymous with predicting political outcomes. Yeah, hard to believe that a county that has forecasted the winning president for seventy years was suddenly wrong when it was Donald Trump's kick at the can, along with all the others except for one.

And how in the world can someone who looked to obviously be in mental decline, that "campaigned" from his basement, only won 1 of 19 bellwether counties, win an election over someone who obtained 11,000,000 more votes than in his previous election; who increased his share of minority voters including Blacks by 50 percent; and who packed arenas, airport hangers, and grandstands throughout the country on a nightly basis to feverous supporters month after month. I don't think he did. Trump's crowd sizes exceeded ten, twenty, and thirty thousand regularly with some of his rallies reportedly exceeding sixty thousand during his run up to the election.

There are only so many things you can claim to be true before even the most unwitting person will start to question your integrity. Hmmm, let's think of a few other examples of obvious attempts to gaslight the general population to convince them that there was no funny business going on in the election. The left would have you believe that Donald J. Trump is a racist who hates everyone that doesn't look like him, but the contrary is evident. He supported all minorities throughout his presidency, and it garnered him gains across all races, with black Americans increasing their support of President Trump by 50 percent going from 8 percent in 2016 to 12 percent in 2020. With all the BS from the Democrats and Joe Biden that has unfolded since then, I bet Donald Trump will garner a lot more minority support in 2024, which seems quite evident in his sweeping victories during the early primaries in Iowa, New Hampshire, Nevada, and South Carolina.

However, the media is reluctant to say the least in disseminating those figures. They are much more comfortable slandering him and at every turn and promoting divisiveness along with anyone who dares to speak out in support of him along the way.

Another interesting anomaly that is regularly hidden away is the extent of voter turnout. After doing some quick research from the past 50 years of election results, it was obvious that voter turnout generally slants on an upward trajectory of approximately 6.5 percent every election cycle with a few outliers here and there. However, according to the federal election results, the number of voters who turned out in 2020 vs 2016 rose by 20 percent! Give me a break! Sounds like a lot of extra counting if you ask me. Donald Trump received an additional 11 million plus votes in 2020 according to the FEC. Many politic analysts indicated that would have secured him the presidency for a second term. One such headline from *Fortune* magazine read, "To win, Trump needs 11 million more votes than he got in 2016."[106] Well, he got them and more! However, it has also been claimed that Joe Biden purportedly received more votes than any other president in history, without even campaigning or coming out of his basement very often. Sounds fishy, if you ask me.

How about campaign strategies? According to the United States Library of Congress, successful candidates must both persuade voters that they deserve their individual votes and garner the critical votes of electors in the Electoral College. Persuading voters is the essence of a "political campaign." Well, keeping that in mind, do you remember how ridiculous Joe Biden's campaigning was? He stayed at home in his basement for the majority of the run up to the election. And when he did get out, he was typically in front of tiny groups of people that on occasion were pushed into circles drawn on the ground. Oh wait ... that was part of the smoke and mirrors used to make the masses believe the only reason we didn't see large crowds was because they were spread out farther and made to stand inside circles for safety. Yeah, we all believed that BS. Meanwhile Donald Trump is crisscrossing the country doing not only many rallies a week but often doing multiples in a single day. Shaking hands and giving away hats in addition to giving one of his classic rally speeches that always brings a crowd of American patriots to its feet in an electrified verve. You won't hear much about that either. I have attended some of those rallies, and let me tell you, the news coverage, if any, is so contradictory, it's hard to believe. They are the most fun and positive experiences you can have. People of all races, ages, and backgrounds attend and unite as Americans, but the left would have you believe they parallel a Hitler rally from the WWII era, with someone at the podium shouting out visceral hatred at the top of his lungs. More gaslighting BS.

Additionally, there have been claims that more votes than voters were cast in certain regions, but these accusations are quickly excused away by saying things like that were in error; or someone put in the wrong number; or there was a software problem. Shortly after the election for example, in four townships in Michigan, there were reportedly 290,000 more votes than voters; however, it was quickly swept under the rug with multiple excuses such as human error or a software setting error occurred. Don't look here. Nothing to see.... Incidents of similar corruption and coverups all across the country were regularly denied and ignored.

Millions turned a blind eye to massive donations and dark money where the DNC and Joe Biden received six times as much money from unknown, large, mega-wealthy donors like George Soros and Fuckerberg. Compare that to the fact that Donald Trump raised more small money donations than Obama, Clinton and Bernie combined.[107] You tell me who will have the interest of the people at heart, and who will have the interest of the mega-corporations ... Additionally, it came out after the election that Fuckerberg gave well over $400,000,000 to aid in getting Joe Biden elected, which significantly exceeds the roughly $3,000 limit.[108] That simply seems against the law, regardless of how they will spin it and attempt to justify that type of behavior through some sort of legal loophole. It makes you wonder what favors he was promised, kick backs he was and will be given, and how absolutely corrupt the system is. It makes me reflect on how certain posts that make the left look bad are quickly taken down, or how a conservative can't easily choose conservative websites as preferences when setting up their computers without Google suggesting a constant barrage of left-wing platforms overtaking your computer. Basically, left wing media and technology companies are controlling what we can and can't see with the support and assistance of the US government. Evidence of this collaboration has become more prevalent over the past couple of years. As well, it looks to continue into the future with policy makers from the Biden administration travelling to the West Coast to consult with social media and tech companies to assist in pointing them in the "right direction" when it comes to artificial intelligence. The world doesn't need another gaslighting source that appears to be genuine and convincing to the general public who believes, "It's on the internet; therefore, it must be true." They don't realize that the AI is still being programed with its initial information by left wing activists.

Let's step back for a moment and reflect on a few examples. I tend to think that anyone regardless of party affiliation would question at least one or two of these things and want them investigated further to get a more comprehensive view of how and why things unfolded as they did in 2020. My common sense tells me by looking at all of these things—and if I take a conservative approach and say, ummm, maybe half are true; maybe a quarter are true; heck maybe just 10 percent are true—then I would say the election results would have certainly come out in a different way and would be worth questioning.

Other examples of gaslighting revolve around the left wing and the arm of the Democrat party major news networks. They cover up for people like Joe Biden and Hillary Clinton, regarding documents and wealth building. You need to look in the right places. But at first glance, you are more likely to see rebuffs of the sort including statements like, "Nothing to see here" or "No evidence of wrong doing" or "No check made out directly to either of them." Such BS! Neither Clinton nor Biden were president until Biden's assignment in 2020; yet they were given what appears to be presidential privilege. The media completely ignores the fact that Joe Biden likely took documents from a SCIF (Sensitive Compartmented Information Facility) when he was a senator and vice president. He simply shouldn't have had or even removed documents from the secured location. Statements like "claims misrepresent 1850 boxes of Biden documents at Delaware University" by the AP are obvious examples of gaslighting to cover up and redirect prying eyes.[109] They also ignore or limit speaking about the millions of dollars of backdoor payments that the Biden family appears to have received from foreign sources and so-called business entities. They received millions of dollars for no apparent services rendered, well, except for the numerous pay-to-play schemes purportedly set up by family members. Why wouldn't the media simply do an audit, ask for tax documents, or follow the money trail (if everything was on the up and up) as they have done endlessly with Donald Trump. That way, they could demonstrate/prove Biden's innocence without looking ridiculous by trying to cover up what appears to be corruption. Apparently, Hunter Biden has received nearly $20 million and counting in foreign payments, and he shares a good portion with the "Big Guy" ... whoever that is ...[110] Gimma a break!

The media has been so blinded by Trump Derangement Syndrome that they are actually starting to believe the crap they are selling to their audience, and ignoring what would typically be very news-worthy stories. The media has unabashedly and willingly exposed their odious thoughts and feelings towards President Trump on a daily basis, and even sometimes an hourly basis, while compromising their ethics and standards of journalism. Not surprisingly mainstream and social media is highly biased and left leaning. A study completed by Research Center's Journalism Project found that fully two-thirds of news stories about Trump from his first sixty days in office were negative by that definition—more than twice the negativity seen in stories from the first sixty days of Bill Clinton, George W. Bush or Barack Obama's presidencies. Meanwhile, only 5 percent of stories about Trump were positive, compared to 42 percent for Obama.[111] Maybe this is because only 7 percent of reporters actually identify as Republicans according to sites like the *Washington Post, Politico*, and *The Daily Beast*. Now, I don't think that you should necessarily have equal representation, but journalists should try to report with less bias and more objectivity. One does have to look at the 7 to 93 percent split and assume that is part of the underlying issue. For people who preach equality, why aren't they addressing that issue? For example, doing a quick search on positive articles related to Donald Trump yields no results, absolutely zero. Interestingly, outside the US, other left leaning countries such as Canada follow suit.

When looking at Canadian news such as government sponsored networks CTV and CBC online, it wasn't surprising to see headlines of each of Donald Trump's indictments, but not one, not even a mention of the investigation into Hunter and Joe Biden's alleged bribery and play-for-pay dealings with Ukraine, China, and beyond. It's as if these things never happened. The 'get Trump' media obsession often drowned out bigger stories like the source of the COVID-19 virus; the media was too busy talking about the Russian Hoax while the pandemic took a back seat—that is of course—until the media spun the story into a racist issue when Donald Trump decided to close the border to China. How dare him! In fact, America's problems still seem to begin and end with Donald Trump, even after his tenure in office. According to the media, he caused the recent power blackouts in Venezuela; his tax-reform plan is destroying the New York state budget; the shooting at the newspaper office in Annapolis was triggered by Trump's toxic environment; and those monsoons wouldn't have happened if Trump hadn't pulled us out of the Paris Climate Accord. All things bad point to Trump!

Even so-called scientific research is biased. Social psychology research will define a Republican as typically not tolerant of others who are different, but they are also more likely to embrace traditional social systems that maintain disparities in wealth and gender, with this theory being more pronounced for Trump supporters. Let's keep in mind that most social psychologists are left leaning. In his 2015 campaign, 70 percent of the $3.9 million he raised from July through September came from people giving $200 or less.[112] Currently Trump has the highest share of small dollar donors, with 82 percent of his funds coming from people who gave $200 or less as I stated above.[113] What does that say?

The mainstream media's habit of missing the big story due to Trump Derangement Syndrome is continuing. At the end of the day, with each indictment, President Trump is becoming a symbol for all of the lower, middle, and working-class Americans and how the government has been screwing us over for years. In fact, the reality is Donald Trump's appeal is becoming more and more diverse as time passes because the America First agenda provides hope, growth, and opportunity for all regardless of your race, color, creed, or national background.

CHAPTER 9

POLITICAL CORRECTNESS AND WOKEISM

Alphabet Soup

"The greatest tyrannies are always perpetrated
in the name of the noblest causes"

- Thomas Paine, Founding Father
1737-1809

Political correctness is a weapon being used by the left to defeat democracy and free speech. It is simply a censoring tool that condemns one group while letting another group dominate speech, and when combined with woke ideology, political correctness becomes a device for manipulating the conscience of the right into submission. Political correctness if allowed to flourish is at the root authoritarian regimes. The term *political correctness* first appeared in Marxist–Leninist vocabulary following the Russian Revolution of 1917.[114] At that time, it was used to describe strict adherence to the policies and principles of the Communist Party of the Soviet Union, that is, the party line. It also aligns with how the Nazis during WWII would only hand out reporting permits to those whose opinions were 'politically correct' in order to 'correctly' relay the information that benefitted their party.

I think before we delve too deeply into how these things are corrupting our world and contributing to TDS, we should define the terms. Political correctness has been described by the *Oxford Reference* as, "the avoidance of forms of expression or action that are perceived to exclude, marginalize, or insult groups of people who are socially disadvantaged or discriminated against."[115] Basically, political correctness changes language with no real, substantive value, as it is more about changing language, censorship, intimidation, and exercising perceived moral purity of those who preach it. Wokeness has been defined as the quality of being alert to injustice (in many cases economic/money based) and discrimination in society, especially racism. However, more recently its spectrum has been broadened by progressive Democrats to encompass and promote identity and racial concepts such as "White privilege," and "reparations to Blacks," and "critical race theory," or "sexual orientation and gender identity."

These ideologies have been around at a basic level for decades, but they have truly blossomed into verbal weapons under millennials and their counterparts who regularly flex these Marxist ideas at their whim. These new world descriptors quickly bristle any conservative as they optimize what the left represents is wrong with western society today. The extreme sensitivity and frailty of those who flagrantly use these terms as offensive mechanisms to censor and control their opposers is relished by most from the left, and when implemented with skill usually make those susceptible, cower in retreat as if they have truly done something wrong.

Living in the western world has given us many opportunities to chase our dreams as we have freedoms afforded to us to be able to pursue life in whatever direction we choose. Sadly, there are those in our current political climate that would like to change how much freedom we have, and/or even eliminate it all together. Proceeding in an insidious fashion, it seems that many on the left have been working towards removing our freedoms by limiting our language and demeaning anyone who doesn't agree with their ideology through the scope of PC culture and woke ideology.

Similarly, it seems the left wing, liberal agenda has been slowly creeping in on normalcy and morality for years, taking what was once a moderate stance and pushing it farther and farther away from the center. It almost seems that on the one hand, they claim to be trying to create an equalized or balanced society through limiting speech and blaming others for miscarriages. At the same time, they are perpetrating biased transgressions against their outgroup thereby continuing to propagate the society of divisiveness and imbalance they claim to be fighting against.

There is an emergence of a culture with extreme sensitivity being created through the use of political correctness and woke ideology that has led to so many claiming that they are victims. The victimology mindset is an extension of PC culture and wokeism that has sadly taken hold of so many.

The PC culture is combined with woke ideology in today's fast-paced world of social media. Heck, all media is greatly contributing to this sickness in our society. On a parallel line of thinking, why and how are the well-minded people of America tolerating the censorship (aka PC culture/wokeism) coming out of the social media platforms. The censorship is implementing all of the guidelines predicated by the PC/woke misfits of our time. These "gurus" of tech are deciding what you can or can't see online (censoring) based on their own hypersensitivity, low self-esteem, and hatred of themselves. These losers have been given an extreme amount of control in our society simply because they were born and educated in a generation when the internet blossomed, and therefore they spent all of their time in front of a computer screen. They target and have a distaste for anyone who is not like them. In their blind, misguided approach, they do what they can to bring down the traditional ideology of a society that they never truly, successfully fit into because of their inept social skills. They limit access to anyone they disapprove because of not following the PC/Woke agenda. That is now the norm, the unwritten agenda of the left. The actions taken against conservatives and Republicans have gone as far as trying to put political opponents in jail because what they are saying is "dangerous."[116] That is simply pure BS and right out of a third world communist country or dictatorship.

These purists are threatened by Donald Trump, as he is the arch nemesis of the PC/Woke culture, and it seems no matter what he says or does, it incites those on the left. His frank common-sense way of speaking is offensive to all of those on the left, starting with the millennials and working its way outward in a rippling effect toward their helicoptering parents, accommodating university professors, and placating media pundits, thereby exacerbating the symptoms of all these TDS sufferers. The extreme sensitivity and perceived moral superiority of those on the left has been taught, and they now unfortunately have the arrogant belief that PC culture and wokeism actually make sense in a real-world way.

Another thorn in the left is Elon Musk, who stated that he believes the operators of Twitter were using woke ideology in "suppressing" those with right wing viewpoints. Thankfully, Musk stepped forward in 2022 by purchasing Twitter and shedding light on the lies, transgressions, and malicious behavior being undertaken by the social media platform. During an interview on a "Podcast with Joe Rogan," Musk stated that he purchased Twitter to stop the "extinctionist" cult that was propagating what he described as a "mind virus."[117]

As his interview with Rogan continued, he went on to say, "This is going to sound somewhat melodramatic, but I was worried it was having a corrosive effect on civilization," He also criticized how the City of San Francisco was being governed, noting that the downtown core was like "a zombie apocalypse." By the way, Twitter has its headquarters in San Francisco. With a rhetorical statement, Musk asked, "So now you have to say, what philosophy led to that outcome?" adding that, "A philosophy that would normally be quite niche and geographically constrained," that being localised to San Francisco, California, or continental US, "was given an information technology weapon to propagate what is essentially a mind virus to the rest of the Earth. And the outcome of that mind virus is very clear if you walk around the streets of downtown San Francisco."

Rogan agreed and described the situation in his own words as a "death cult." The two went on discussing the topic with Musk agreeing with Rogan by stating yes, "It's essentially the extinctionists. It is that they're propagating the extinction of humanity and civilization." On other numerous occasions, Musk has also described it as a "woke mind virus" when describing left wing thinking. In December of 2022, Musk proclaimed on X, that the "woke mind virus is either defeated or nothing else matters." And earlier in the year he stated, "there needs to be a counter-narrative" as woke ideology has also, "thoroughly penetrated entertainment." Maybe the counter narrative, is the cure to TDS!

This is what I have been talking about. Musk has hit the nail on the head when describing woke/PC BS. This is not surprising as he is likely one of the most intelligent people in the world today. Musk is the ultimate twenty-first century industrialist who has founded the world-renowned SpaceX, Telsa, and is the savior of X; is worth hundreds of billions of dollars, and has a clear and intelligent evaluation of the current global mindset. His IQ must be off the charts!

Speaking about IQs, let's look at what has been happening over the last few decades that may be a contributing factor to progressive ideology and TDS. Lower IQ, maybe? James Flynn, an intelligence researcher, studied the trend of IQs over many years, and subsequently some of his research findings were named after him, "The Flynn Effect." The Flynn Effect displays historical evidence of a steadily increasing IQ of the general population over numerous decades until about the 1990s.[118] People were generally becoming smarter and scoring better on standardized tests. However, in the 90s a pause/reversal began to take hold, with IQ scores of the more recent generations actually stagnating or becoming lower.[119] There is speculation as to why the reversal has occurred, but for the sake of this argument, why it's happening is not as important as the fact that it *is* happening. This is pure speculation on my part, but it is logical to assume that an individual with a lower IQ would have more difficulty understanding, adapting, and fluidly being able to rationalize a situation or concept, therefore leading to their becoming uncomfortable. This discomfort could easily lead to a counterattack in an attempt—out of shear ignorance—to shut down the person, thought, or belief that makes them uncomfortable … aka cancel culture. It is my belief that the PC/woke culture is responsible for this trend as these ideologies promote shutting down the mind rather than engaging in critical thinking, research and discourse, and focusing instead on their emotions, which ultimately limits their ability to intellectually move forward.

Additionally, rather than think things through or debate differences, the left seems prone to exercising their opinions through violence. An example is the rioting taking place across the USA in the turbulent times prior to the 2020 presidential election, during the Chinese virus pandemic, COVID 19. There was complete disregard for keeping everyone safe from transmitting the virus by avoiding assembling in large groups, and carrying out acts of violence and destruction without concern of who it may be impacting. This was happening on a daily basis in some parts of the country. I have travelled to many of these cities in the past, but will not likely be doing that in the near future unless things dramatically change. The rioting and violence that has been taking place in liberal-run cities—such as New York, Philadelphia, Chicago, Portland, Seattle, and San Francisco to name a few—is destroying these once wonderful cities.[120] It is absolutely appalling, and making them incredibly dangerous. This lack of leadership and delinquent behavior of the few are classic manifestations of the egocentric, spoiled child, and are contributing to increasing the homeless population and creating a circular trap of poverty, crime, drug use, violence, and death.

Much of this behavior has purportedly been initiated and carried out in the fight against racism and fascism, and all the other BS the PC/WOKE culture is blaming on the world. These proclamations are utterly absurd, not to say that racism, fascism or Marxism don't exist in the world today, but not to the degree that rises to an attempted overthrow of the current form of democracy. Common sense is unwarranted regarding the exaggerated form of millennials' displeasure which has culminated in a frenzied group tantrum.

I recently watched Heisman Trophy winner (and yes, great NFL player) Hershel Walker declaring to those who are not happy in this country, that perhaps that should leave. He even tweeted that he was willing to work with major US airlines to provide flights for those who are unhappy in the USA, so they could travel to a place that does not have law and order, so they could be happy. [121] His tweet read:

"I have an idea … For all these people who don't want any police, I'd love to meet with American Airlines, Delta, and Southwest and make a deal to fly those folks to countries that don't have police. I want them to be happy!"

He was prompted by what his son Christian tweeted earlier:

"My dad grew up in the deep south as a poor, black man and turned himself into a notable athlete, business man, and person," Christian Walker wrote. "No, I don't feel bad for 'oppressed' people who run around burning buildings down. I'm not sorry I'm grateful for my country/the opportunities it's given me."[122]

I totally agree with what both of these gentlemen are saying. Basically, if you don't like it here, don't let the door hit you on the ass! These men were obviously raised to believe in the American way; they are great patriots and not vulnerable or succumbing to the PC/woke culture insanity.

Another example of the left's ideology was on display as I was watching the news. I witnessed a young person in Portland, Oregon being detained by officers without name tags or badges. The left wing pundits were very upset regarding this incident, stating that it was against the Constitution and an infringement on that person's rights to be detained by someone who was not identified.

Well, the left seems to very often conveniently forget to mention things: In this case the person who was detained was wearing paramilitary gear; was leaving the immediate area of a riot; and was observed consorting with others to undertake illegal activities. Well, if it looks like a duck, swims like a duck, and quacks like a duck, then it is probably a duck. Oh, did I mention this person wasn't wearing a name tag that said, "My name is … and I'm with Antifa?" No, of course he wasn't wearing or carrying any identifying information. Most criminals don't. Obviously, these individuals are not completely void of intellect, as they have likely found a way of being funded by wealthy people like Soros; they have figured out how to coordinate via the internet and smart phone applications to maintain relative anonymity; how to protect themselves in aggressive situations by wearing protective gear and bringing nondescript weaponry and raising their hands when confronted by authorities. When all of these factors are combined with the politically correct woke culture and subsequent hand tying of policing agencies, it becomes very difficult to have a reasonable and just outcome.

The left wing has realized that conservatives have morality, know right from wrong, and don't easily cross those boundaries, and with that information in mind they have the ability to manipulate and push farther than would normally be expected as there are no serious repercussions. It's like fighting an army that doesn't wear a uniform and doesn't follow any code of conduct. Those on the left who constantly preach about PC culture and woke ideology are simply nothing more than 'Morality Terrorists'

These destructive people have gained insight in how to manipulate the law and conscience of the right. What is truly a shame, is that in the long run, it seems as if the few, the so called 'squeaky wheel' will get the grease, and the majority of the people in the country will simply grin and bear it regardless of how they truly feel. Perhaps it is out of fear of being ridiculed or attacked in today's bullying culture?

One person who dared to speak out was Bernell Trammell. This man was shot and killed outside of his business in Milwaukee for supporting

President Trump.[123] Oh yeah, by the way Mr. Trammell also happened to be a sixty-year-old black man. I wonder why BLM didn't protest the loss of his life? This is just one of many examples of violence perpetrated by the left and swept under the rug by those who should be speaking out. What about Aaron Danielson being shot and killed in Portland Oregon by an attendee and self-proclaimed security guard of the BLM/Antifa movements?[124] Danielson had attended a pro-Trump rally earlier in the day and was apparently targeted, shot, and killed because of his perpetrator's indoctrination into the PC/woke world of stupidity.

Another example is from November 2023, as I'm writing this and listening to the news on how another person, Jonathan Lewis, a seventeen-year-old student who was defending a smaller friend was killed by a group of fifteen teenagers.[125] These f*!*#'s ganged up on him, punching and kicking him in a frenzy of animalistic blows. Obviously, these individuals have no sense of morality, no proper parenting, no school or civic leadership, and are free to run around like animals doing whatever they want. PC culture, wokeism, divisiveness, envy, hatred toward police, and a lack of leadership are all empowering these so-called 'victims' to tear down society. These disgusting animals along with their parents should be charged and put away for a long time. But more than likely, the most they will incur will be a slap on the wrist, and no one in the media will point out how heinous this action was as it doesn't fit today's narrative. Someone needs to be held responsible and put a stop to the madness of the PC culture!

I believe that these left wing ideological principles are born out of the ignorance of a coddled generation who have no individuality, can't think independently, and have a desire to fabricate "causes," to have their own cause in order to give themselves purpose. It's like becoming an arsonist to increase the need for firefighters. The likely distaste for PC culture and language besides the obvious is that it hasn't evolved naturally/organically in society over time, but has rather been thrust upon the masses by a select few on the left in an attempt to leave their mark on history of being morally "superior" to the rest of us.

I also suspect that the lack of leadership in western cultures in the form of power grabbing cabals is a major contributor utilizing PC culture and woke ideology to achieve their goals, thereby exacerbating TDS. Hillary Clinton's lack of leadership of the Democrat Party after her 2016 defeat has likely contributed not surprisingly to conflict, low morale and motivation, resistance to change, and an unwillingness toward responsibility within the electorate that desired her success. The appearance of her selfishness, narcissism, and self-indulgent behavior is likely one of the major antagonists to the exacerbation of TDS in society today. She reminds me of a spoiled child who didn't get her way, has been throwing a tantrum ever since, and has been dragging the Democrat Party down with her.

More recently Joe Biden, just a few years after he left office as vice president, attempted to take credit for what Donald Trump just accomplished.[126] I'm referring to the 2020, deal brokered between the UAE, Bahrain, and Israel (the Abraham Accord) which Donald Trump orchestrated through Jared Kushner, the president's son-in-law.[127] Joe Biden's denial of reality, and his grasp at Donald Trump's achievement is another example of his poor leadership capability. Joe Biden along with his president Barack Obama attempted to foster a wider Arab-Israel opening, but forgot one critical component, respect for Israel. Harvard Law Professor Alan Dershowitz described Obama's "deep hatred of Israel."[128] Biden and Obama have criticized Israel, and at one point Joe Biden even criticized their housing policy in Jerusalem. I am not going to get into global policy here, but I certainly can identify poor leadership when I see it.

And then there is Barack Husein Obama.... He disparaged half the country because they don't see things his way. It has also been suggested numerous times that he is still trying to contribute in leading the country from behind the scenes with Joe Biden being his puppet. On the one hand, he believes in affirmative action, helping the impoverished, while on the other hand he lives in a multi-million-dollar mansion on Martha's Vineyard and seemingly does nothing to assist the very people he preached about helping. It appears that he has cognitive dissonance regarding how he should be leading his life.

Contributing to the dysfunction, the media has somehow lost there way. They are no longer unbiased, no longer seem to verify information, and are basically an arm of the DNC. Over the past several years, numerous US cities have started to move in a negative direction. they are in disrepair, operating over budget with crime going up and employment going down. A majority of these cities have been led by Democrat political figures that have little interest in improving the quality of life for its inhabitants. That said, it seems that these politicians have been getting a pass from broad swaths of the media. I sat dumbfounded in front of my television listening to reporters and commentators saying that the protests of 2020 were peaceful, with limited-to-no crime taking place at all. Meanwhile, I am watching people being beaten and businesses being destroyed, in what I would describe as a society on the brink of anarchy.

People like Mayor Adams of New York are telling people to do things like breath and limit meat consumption while that city is being tormented with homelessness, violence, and crime of all kinds.[129] It looks like the leadership is out of touch with reality. He was very likely elected because of his more than twenty years of working with the police. His constituents probably thought he was going to be a little tougher on crime. That is not how he has conducted himself. And now he is disenchanted to say the least regarding how illegal immigrants are overtaking his city. But hey, you signed up as a sanctuary city ... no?

Sanctuary cities. Let's take a closer look. Illegal immigrants are over burdening cities and towns, unfortunately taking support away from US citizens. The softening of laws, (e.g., no cash bail, no criminal charge for thefts of $1,000) is another ridiculous decision by local politicians in sanctuary cities which is amplifying the problem.[130] The crime rates are going up, but the offenders are not being held accountable. And as anyone knows, to deter bad behavior, the offender must be held accountable. When visiting these cities, it reminds me of third world countries, the kinds of places people try to escape. The surprising part is that the left supports this civic decay, and displays a lack of support for Americans who truly need help, like our veterans. Nothing good will likely happen at this point. And undoubtedly, violence will continue; people will die, and others will go to jail. It's simply ridiculous. All of that could be avoided if the elected politicians did their jobs, enforced common sense laws, and aided their citizens, instead of siding with people who are in fact breaking the law by simply being in the country, robbing our stores, and by littering the streets with themselves after getting strung out on drugs.

So many politicians would rather let the US crumble out of spite towards Donald J. Trump. I do find it priceless how the politicians of our country have been using illegals as chess pieces being moved around the country rather than owning up to their mistakes. Their inability to face facts is just another symptom of TDS. For example, how many times have we heard the so-called elite say that we should *allow in as many illegals as possible because after all they just want a better life.*

But when Governor Abbott started shipping illegals to the northeast, everyone's tune started changing. And they only seem fine with that concept as long as another state takes care of the illegals. Hypocritical! Their TDS is going to create difficult-to-inhabit regions spattered across the country where only the criminal element remains—or those without the means to leave. A survivalist mentality will prevail, and people will die. And all of this is due to the decision-makers' inability to admit that their hasty decisions were wrong. These so called 'politicians of the people' are obviously willing to let their citizens, cities, states, and country go down the tubes rather than to admit their wrongdoing and accept the fact that rules and laws are beneficial in maintaining society in a functional and safe manner for the majority of the population. One thing this democracy has taught most rational non-TDS-suffering individuals: Regardless of your political slant, most everyone generally wants to work together for the good of the country. Obviously both Democrats and Republicans have their agendas, and in the past, they have been able to find some sort of middle ground. However, since the emergence of TDS, it seems that those afflicted are unwilling or possibly unable to make what most of us would deem to be *rational* decisions. It's more of a *must-win-at-all-costs mentality*. When I say *unable*, I presume that they are seriously overwhelmed by TDS and have not yet sought out the appropriate treatment.

How about the Biden appointee Pete Buttigieg, aka Alfred E. Neuman…. This guy seems to take off more time than Joe Biden, and that's no small feet. He is supposed to be the nineteenth United States Secretary of Transportation, but he takes two months off for maternity leave during a critical time. Well, I think its time for him to reconsider his area of expertise. How many screwups can this obviously unqualified guy make? Even a knucklehead rookie gets things right once in awhile, just by chance. The supply chain breakdown under him was unprecedented. Wonder why you don't have baby formula? Call Mayor Pete. Between the two-year backlog of freighters off the West Coast, by 2022, there were even more stacked up on the East Coast with reports exceeding 600,000 containers waiting to be offloaded.[131] Okay, okay, maybe ships aren't his thing. Well, what about not addressing the rail disaster in East Palestine for an extended period with what can only be described as a canned lukewarm response. Maybe he will have better luck if we look to the skies … *nope,* airline cancellations and delays are more regular than ever. "What we got here … is … failure to communicate."

Then, of course, there is Joe Biden … how do I count the ways. Oh my God … there isn't enough paper in the world to print that list. From leaving Afghanistan the way he did, shuttering the XL Pipeline, the two-tiered justice system, inflation, the border, apparently hijacking papers as a senator, and how about all the constant mistruths and hair sniffing.[132] That behavior is just weird! But really, more seriously, how can this guy go on two back-to-back vacations with one being at the beach, and ignore the fact that a good portion of Hawaii was burning, and people were dying during the horrific fire in the summer of 2023. What was that … No comment … Where is this guy's humanity? And, on top of all that is his use of aliases, numerous bank accounts, and a swath of what appear to be shell businesses …[133]

Perhaps I cannot blame everything on TDS, as our world seems to have been going mad for some time. Now I sound like my parents, and yours too more than likely, as every generation seems to disapprove of the following one. However, the turn of the millennium or thereabouts seems to have added fuel, growing the PC culture exponentially to the point of insanity. "The meek shall inherit the earth" seems to be upon us. The inflammatory declarations over just about anything someone says has given power to the meek and the masses through the anonymity of today's technology, which is unpresented and harmful to our society. You're a racist, sexist, xenophobe, etc…

The media and popular culture are also to blame. The constant barrage of negative comments directed at the opposing party and its supporters is bound to have repercussions. Look at the programs that have been cancelled just because they were right leaning like Tucker Carlson (highest rated primetime program across all cable channels), *Lou Dobbs Tonight* (the most watched business show of the year), and the Tim Allen show *Last Man Standing* (the highest-rated, scripted comedy). These programs were in their respective number 1 slot bringing in more viewers, and presumably more revenue, so why would they get cancelled? The infliction of Trump Derangement Syndrome causes once rational people to make the most ludicrous decisions. How many viewers do you think they lost by cancelling number 1 rated shows, and on a supposed conservative network. So why do it? Because they hate Trump and don't want to encourage common sense conservative ideology. In fact, they would like to do just the opposite, and that is why we have been seeing so many organizations make poor business decisions. Budweiser comes to mind …

Trump has been a lightning rod since entering the arena of politics. He has been a symbol for all Americans, for those hard working who don't ask much but a fair wage; for those with grander dreams of creating million-dollar companies; for those who believe in law and order and nationalism and security for themselves and their family, and for all of those new Americans who came here the proper way. Because of this he also symbolises a significant threat to the corrupt political establishment who, for many generations, have benefited from their political position. These wolves have spearheaded a campaign to tear him and his movement down, ripping the flesh from the bones of anyone who dares to support him, as he and his supporters are standing in the way of their continued wealth accumulation, power, and corruption.

We have seen the lefts use of extensive manipulation in the form of gaslighting with an attempt to regulate and restrict our language, aka PC culture and wokeism to control our behavior under the guise of social justice. These tools have been used in the hope of extinguishing Donald Trump and the MAGA movement, but they only served to illuminate the depth of Trump Derangement Syndrome.

CHAPTER 10

MAKE AMERICA GREAT AGAIN

…Not gold but only men can make
A people great and strong;
Men who for truth and honor's sake
Stand fast and suffer long.

Brave men who work while others sleep,
Who dare while others fly…
They build a nation's pillars deep

And lift them to the sky.

- William Ralph Emerson
1833-1917

What is Trump Derangement Syndrome? It is a disorder derived from the dysfunctional aspect of the hippie generation, through the millennials and their parents, propagated by social media, and culminated by extreme liberal left wing ideology, orchestrated by the deep state, and proliferated through means of groupthink, wokeism, and gaslighting. Liberal characteristics such as external locus of control, envy, narcissism, weak moral development, and low self-confidence, combined with a lack of leadership have all exacerbated the development of TDS, allowing it to flourish in the minds of the weak and vulnerable.

The deep state powers have orchestrated a campaign to paint Donald Trump as an evil man and a threat to democracy, where in fact he is threatening to drain their swamp. Trump has the power of the people, with a commanding influence, which is why the left fears him so. The propaganda machine includes the deep state, legacy media, entertainers, big tech, and Hollywood all churning out not only negative, but vile and hateful schemas of Trump, his family, and his supporters. The blind acceptance of these spiteful, vindictive descriptions of this man were the first step towards the development of the maladaptive behaviors we now know as Trump Derangement Syndrome. Social media became the catalyst for groupthink and bullying, while generational factors have exacerbated Democrat traits and the psychological underpinnings of liberalism-fueled TDS.

But the question remains. Is TDS a true diagnosable disorder? We suspect that an individual with true TDS can actually be diagnosed with what is called an 'adjustment disorder' according to the DSM-5. An adjustment disorder displays marked distress that is out of proportion to the severity or intensity of the stressor and can involve negative thoughts, strong emotions, and changes in behavior. These criteria certainly seem to be met by a great number of left-leaning individuals in America today.

The left has exhibited an inability to accept Donald Trump as president of the United States, and the fact that a minimum of 71 million people voted for him simply can't be denied by a healthy, rational person. Certainly, the inability to adjust and accept his successes are signs of the initial manifestations of TDS. The liberals have clearly demonstrated a loss of decorum, civility, and common sense with anything related to Trump. He is the worst thing they can imagine, and in their mind, he must be destroyed. Since President Trump has announced his candidacy for the 2024 Presidential election, TDS has blown up once again. We have witnessed never ending accusations, impeachments, and charges against him because of TDS.

Trump is an outsider, which is the biggest threat to the corrupt, ruling class establishment, and as former speaker of the house, Newt Gingrich said, "And they learned from watching Donald Trump that a true outsider, willing to take on the entire system could destroy their entire machine. So, what you're seeing across the country, is the desperate, last-ditch effort of the corrupt machine to destroy their most dangerous opponent in a way which not only breaks the Constitution, destroys the rule of law, and establishes a moment of bitterness that I think will last for a generation or more."[134]

Professor Victor Davis Hanson remarked that when Donald Trump on November 15, 2022, declared his intention to run for the Republican presidential nomination in 2024, he was faced with, as Professor Hanson described, "a cohort of weaponized left wing prosecutors." Indeed, as the indictments continue to stack up, Joe Biden has been given de facto exemptions. The aim is clearly to banish, isolate, and to monopolize Trump's time and money, and to impede his campaigning in 2023 and 2024.[135] The indictment of a former president in undeniably historical, never mind four times!

Let's recall, Trump has faced a range of criminal and civil investigations since he announced his run for presidency in 2015. He has been subjected to two impeachment trials, the 2016 election "Russian collusion" hoax, and the September 2019 "the perfect phone call" impeachment to President Zelensky, and now he is facing ninety-one criminal charges across four jurisdictions—Georgia, Florida, New York, and the District of Columbia involving allegations of attempted election theft, hush money payments, and mishandling classified documents. Majority leader Chuck Schumer warned Trump, "Let me tell you, you take on the intelligence community, they have six ways from Sunday at getting back at you," he told MSNBC's Rachel Maddow.[136] Low and behold on August 8, 2022, it was underway—the FBI raid of Trump's residence at his Mar-a-Lago beach club in Palm Beach related to an investigation into the handling of National Archives (NA) records that were taken to the Florida residence after he left office. It is the first time a former US president's home has ever been searched by law enforcement. Another first. This was an obvious attempt to intimidate, discredit, and set up Donald Trump through an exploratory fishing trip looking for evidence to intimidate and charge him with just about anything and/or possible in an attempt to recover incriminating evidence against the deep state that he may have had in his possession. The abuse of power utilized to condemn a man who was once the president of the United States is unprecedented, and was a display that showed the average person that they should be fearful of the current political regime as they have indomitable power that they are not afraid of using against anyone who opposes them.

Lindsey Halligan, a lawyer for President Trump, said she had received a call around 10:00 a.m. local time that the FBI had a search warrant for Mar-a-Lago and that she should come to the property.[137] She said she saw thirty to forty gloved FBI agents, some in suits and others dressed casually, and around ten to fifteen FBI vehicles, including a rental truck. Ms. Halligan told CBS she and another lawyer for President Trump were barred from entering the complex at that time. President Trump stated that they ultimately broke into his safe and searched his wife's closet. Former FBI agent Stewart Kaplan said, "This is so overdone and heavy-handed; it just is shameful. They went in there, and they were able to look under every nook and cranny. That's called a fishing expedition. That's improper. That's un-American and that's not what the FBI is all about." Kaplan said after reading the affidavit, he feels the FBI was politically weaponized in this case and that the intrusive search of Mar-a-Lago cannot be justified.[138]

The two-tier justice system is alive and well in the US. President Trump may go to prison for removing White House files to his home, but Joe Biden seems exempt despite as a senator and vice president with no right when compared to a president, to declassify files; had for years kept classified files in his Delaware garage next to his prized Corvette. In another example, as Professor Victor David Hanson said, President Trump was impeached by a Democratic House for "delaying foreign aid until the Ukrainian government guaranteed that Hunter Biden and his family were no longer engaged in corrupt influence peddling in Kyiv."[139] Yet as we have seen umpteen times, Biden bragged about firing a Ukrainian prosecutor looking into Hunter's schemes by promising to "cancel outright American foreign aid."[140] The apparent corrupt Biden family is currently being investigated by the Republicans, with significant receipts including cashed checks of significant amounts; however, the media continues to declare there is no evidence of their corruption. Look! Look over here ... Trump may have inflated his Mar-a-Lago property value. Let's destroy his business in New York along with his family, despite no evidence of malfeasance, with witnesses denying all claims made by the left, and loans that were paid back in full. The witch hunt continues!

Trump was indicted by Special Counsel Jack Smith, for allegedly unlawfully discounting legitimate votes.[141] Atlanta DA Fani Willis files a massive slate of RICO indictments against Donald Trump and eighteen alleged co-conspirators of Trump. It basically seeks to criminalize any effort to dispute the 2020 election on a federal or state level. This should preclude the local DA from filing this indictment; however, the leftist mob does what it wants, having one set of laws for themselves and another for everyone else. I guess its okay for Georgia House Representative Stacey Abrams, who falsely claimed that she was the real governor of Georgia, who had hopes of 'discounting' the state vote count.[142]

Or maybe if you are Hillary Clinton who said: Trump, "knows he's an illegitimate president. I believe he understands that the many varying tactics they used, from voter suppression and voter purging, to hacking, to the false stories—he knows that—there were just a bunch of different reasons why the election turned out like it did ... I know he knows this wasn't on the level."[143] In an October 2020 interview with *The Atlantic,* Clinton said, "There was a widespread understanding that the 2016 election was not on the level. We still don't know what happened ... but you don't win by 3 million votes and have all this other shenanigans and stuff going on and not come away with an idea like, 'Whoa, something's not right here."[144] Or how about in January 2005, thirty-two Democrat House members and California Senator Barbara Boxer tried to nullify the legally certified vote in Ohio. I guess it is okay to denounce election results only if you are a Democrat.[145]

Professor Victor Davis Hanson said, "We have now serially devolved from the 2016 election 'Russian collusion' hoax, to the 2020 election 'Russian disinformation' laptop hoax, and down to the 2024 election weaponized indictments." This is a result "out of pathological hatred or fear of Donald Trump (AKA: TDS). As he concludes that, "They smugly believe their own moral superiority grants them such a right to apply laws unequally," a clear example of TDS and as previously discussed, collective narcissism.[146]

And of course, there is January 6, 2021. The Chief of Capital Police, Steven Sund, in an interview with Tucker Carlson on X, whose requests for support made on January 3 were denied. Lawmakers investigating January 6th tried to prevent Sund from testifying and kept Nancy Pelosi 'off limits.' The assistant chief for intelligence Yogananda Pittman of the Capitol Police was absolved of responsibility. Interestingly, Sund noted that when Pelosi promoted Yogananda Pittman as acting chief, she received a "vote of no confidence," but now serves as chief of police at the University of California at Berkeley, most likely courtesy of Nancy Pelosi. Sund also detailed how soldiers were not allowed to go to the Capitol until after "the fight's over" at 6:00 p.m. noting the New Jersey State Police arrived at the Capitol before the National Guard.

As the man himself, Donald Trump said on Truth Social on November 13, 2023:

> "Deranged Jack Smith, Andrew Weissman, Lisa Monaco, the "team of losers and misfits" from CREW, and all of the rest of the Radical Left Zealots and Thugs who have been working illegally for years to "take me down" will end up, because of their suffering from a horrible disease, Trump Derangement Syndrome (TDS!) in a mental institution by the time my next term as President is successfully completed."

President Trump has certainly identified the depth to which TDS has 'flourished.' His identification of the flourishing syndrome is verified through the resurgence of TDS to a fever pitch which can more recently be seen in the actions of the left leading up to the 2024 election. Biden's campaign even released 2023 Thanksgiving talking points for "crazy Maga nonsense."[147] In other words, they want their minions to start discussing politics around the dinner table to either recalibrate what they describe as 'hateful thoughts' of MAGA supporters or to create dissension and divisiveness within families. TDS is in full view when House Democrat Daniel Goldman of New York, while being interviewed on a nationally broadcasted program, stated that Donald Trump should be "eliminated."[148] Then there is the Univision story. Donald Trump was the first Republican president to be interviewed on the network in over twenty years, and of course, once again it stirred up a controversy. A number of left wing extremists, including the congressional Democrat Hispanic Caucus stated that the interview was unfair, didn't push back against Trump enough, and should have never taken place. Additionally, a call to boycott the network ensued.[149]

Even more extreme than the previous two examples are the blue states attempts to ban Donald Trump's name from even appearing on the primary and general election ballots. "It's outrageous, egregious, preposterous!" aptly said by the Seinfeld character Jackie Chiles. The left is so full of BS! They laugh at Trump, make fun and demean him; then they say *we want to run against him as he will be easy to beat.* Then they try to impeach and criminalize him to make his supporters hate him and take away his ability to run. And, when they failed at all of that and realized they are only making support for him grow stronger, and are broadening his base, they try to have his named removed from the ballot altogether. All of these calls to action against Trump smack of desperation, and lead me to believe that there is another "October Surprise" around the corner, waiting to be dropped on the American public in a Hail Mary attempt to de-thrown the last American hero just moments before the election.

The left is doing a full court press as if the time clock is running down, and they only have moments left to "win their game." What was once a glacial pace of a tectonic shift toward a free society evolving naturally, has more recently been thrust into overdrive toward a socialist society with no boundaries. The slow, incessant changes have been accelerated. Javier Milei, the recently elected Argentinian President, reminded me of an old metaphor based on Sorites Paradox, which in this case reflects on creeping normality. The metaphor is about frogs in a pot of boiling water, and he aligned it with what has been happening in many cultures for years around the world including North America. The theory is that if you put live frogs in a pot of water, and begin to heat it at a very slow rate, that the frogs will not notice, and will eventually die from the extreme temperature, but if you throw live frogs into a boiling pot of water, they will jump out right away as they most certainly notice the dramatic change in temperature. In other words, the more gradually something takes place, the higher the likelihood it will go unnoticed. This is why I believe the left has succeeded in pushing their agendas this far. With Donald Trump becoming president, they have been shocked into experiencing TDS.

Is treatment available for those inflicted? Maybe a cure? How can we help people that are suffering from this syndrome? Is there treatment or a cure for TDS that is aptly described as an adjustment disorder? Can the victims of TDS recover? Will they ever be able to move on and have a normal productive life beyond their obsession with Donald Trump? I believe so, but it will take time. As with any syndrome, many factors will play a role in recovery. I highly doubt that many will self-identify with this syndrome, but keep in mind, the earlier one accepts that they are struggling and begins treatment, the better the prognosis.

Typically, the removal of the stressor will alleviate the symptoms of TDS, but fortunately there is no taking down the most resilient man on earth! He isn't going anywhere, and hopefully he will become the forty-seventh President of the United States of America. We are witnessing a severe exacerbation of the symptoms as the election approaches; there are small signs of common sense and a realization that Donald Trump is not a threat, but given the state of the country, he is actually more like a savior, and will hopefully rise to the top once again becoming the 47th president of the United States!

We have come to understand that liberals are more likely to have an external locus of control, have more difficulties in adapting to change, and are more susceptible to experiencing negative envy, moral clarity, groupthink, misandrist attitudes, and are likely to use tools such as gaslighting to drive political correctness and wokeism down the throat of anyone who stands in their way. When allowed to manifest these maladjusted methods of thinking with like-minded individuals who reinforce their misguided beliefs, they become a formidable foe of common sense, rationality, and democracy as a whole.

In fact, the reality is that the MAGA movement is becoming more and more diverse because the America First agenda provides hope, growth, and opportunity for all. Maybe, just maybe, the left can see that Trump and his supporters are not misogynist, racist, homophobic, antisemitic, or hateful, but rather that he and his supporters believe in family, faith, freedom, and the American way.

ENDNOTES

CHAPTER 1

1. DSM History. (n.d.). American Psychiatric Association. Retrieved August 1, 2022, from https://www.psychiatry.org/psychiatrists/practice/dsm/about-dsm/history-of-the-dsm

2. Lustig,R.H. (2018b, July 26). This Is Your Brain on Trump. MEDPAGETODAY. https://www.medpagetoday.com/psychiatry/generalpsychiatry/74232

3. Graham, L. (2019, December 19). *Whether you agree with impeachment or not, Trump Derangement Syndrome has reached a new level. House Democrats refusing to send the Articles of Impeachment to the Senate because they don't like the way we may do the trial – that is just scary.* X. https://twitter.com/LindseyGrahamSC/status/1207743401036308480

4. *GOP REP diagnoses top House Judiciary chair with "Trump derangement Syndrome" -Then turns to the camera.* (2019). Pluralist. https://pluralist.com/matt-gaetz-jerry-nadler/

5. Trump, D. (2020, February 27). *"Anti-Trump Network @CNN doing whatever it can to stoke a national Coronavirus panic. The far left Network pretty much ignoring anyone who they interview who doesn't blame President Trump."* @trish_regan.X. https://twitter.com/realDonaldTrump/status/1233208695099666433?ref_src=twsrc%5Etfw%7Ctwcamp%5E tweetembed%7Ctwterm%5E1233208695099666433%7Ctwgr%5Ef1dc364411ccdaae0d 7dc34badffea6612a5b94d%7Ctwcon%5Es1_&ref_url=https%3A%2F%2Fwww.mediaite. com%2Fnews%2Fthe-day-trump-was-reportedly-briefed-about-russian-bounties-trump-hit-back-hard-at-cnn%2F

6. Sexton, B. (2020, January 20). *Blaming Trump for Iran shooting a civilian airliner out of its own airspace while committing an act of war against both America and Iraq-may be the closest we have come to isolating the virus that causes Trump Derangement Syndrome.* X.

7. Carr, H. (2017, January 4). Trump Derangement Syndrome Reaches Epidemic Levels. *Boston Herald.* https://www.bostonherald.com/2017/01/04/carr-trump-derangement-syndrome-reaches-epidemic-levels/

8. Many Americans Stressed About the Future of our Nation, New APA Stress in America Survey Reveals. (2017). *American Psychological Association.* https://www.apa.org/news/press/releases/2017/02/stressed-nation

9. Kim, Y. S. (2016, November 9). Devasted Cornellians "Mourn" Election of Donald Trump at Cry In *The Cornell Daily Sun.* https://cornellsun.com/2016/11/09/devastated-cornellians-mourn-election-of-donald-trump-at-cry-in/

10. Singman, B. (2016, November 17). Coddling campus crybabies: Students take up toddler therapy after Trump win. *Fox News.* https://www.foxnews.com/us/coddling-campus-crybabies-students-take-up-toddler-therapy-after-trump-win

11. Messing, D. (2019, August 30). *Please print a list of all attendees please. The public has a right to know.* Twitter.

12. Rosenblatt, K. (2017, May 31). Kathy Griffin Fired by CNN over Gruesome Photo of Trump. *NBC News.* https://www.nbcnews.com/news/us-news/kathy-griffin-fired-cnn-over-gruesome-photo-trump-n766716

CHAPTER 2

13. *Rotter, Julian B (1966). "Generalized expectancies for internal versus external control of reinforcement". Psychological Monographs: General and Applied. 80 (1): 1–28. doi:10.1037/ h0092976. PMID 5340840. S2CID 15355866.*

14. Molinari V, Khanna P. Locus of control and its relationship to anxiety and depression. J Pers Assess. 1981 Jun;45(3):314-9. doi: 10.1207/s15327752jpa4503_14. PMID: 7252756.

15. Can having internal locus of control insure against negative shocks ? Psychological evidence from panel data. (2016, February). *Journal of Economic Behavior & Organization, 122,* 88–109. https://www.sciencedirect.com/science/article/abs/pii/S0167268115003108

16. Ibid.

17. Golding J, Gregory S, Ellis GL, Iles-Caven Y, Nowicki S. Prenatal Internal Locus of Control Is Positively Associated with Offspring IQ, Mediated through Parenting Behavior, Prenatal Lifestyle and Social Circumstances. Front Psychol. 2017 Aug 22;8:1429. doi: 10.3389/ fpsyg.2017.01429. PMID: 28878722; PMCID: PMC5572283.

18. Schneewind, K. Λ. (1995). Impact of family processes on control beliefs. In A. Bandura (Ed.), *Self-efficacy in changing societies* (pp. 114–148). Cambridge University Press. https:// doi.org/10.1017/CBO9780511527692.006*Theories of Personality* (11th ed.). (2015). [Print]. Cengage Learning.

19. *If you are not a liberal at 25, you have no heart. If you are not a conservative at 35 you have no brain.* (2014, February 24). Quote Investigator. https://quoteinvestigator. com/2014/02/24/heart-head/

20. Gollwitzer, Mario. (2021). Matters arising from Gabay, R., Hameiri, B., Rubel-Lifschitz, R., & Nadler, A. (2020). The tendency for interpersonal victimhood: The personality construct and its consequences. Personality and Individual Differences, 165, 110134. Personality and Individual Differences. 168. 110294. 10.1016/j.paid.2020.110294.

21. B Kaufman, S. (2020, June 29). *Unraveling the mindset of victimhood*. Scientific American. https://www.scientificamerican.com/article/unraveling-the-mindset-of-victimhood/

22. Nagarubini Paramasivam1*, & Yohan Kurniawan2 , Fairuz a'dilah3. (2023, June). THE DEFENCE MECHANISMS USED BY HYSTERIA MALAY STUDENTS IN KELANTAN TO PROTECT THEMSELVES FROM UNCOMFORTABLE BEHAVIOURS. *INTERNATIONAL JOURNAL OF EDUCATION, PSYCHOLOGY AND COUNSELLING (IJEPC), 8*(50). http://www.ijepc.com/PDF/ IJEPC-2023-50-06-13.pdf

23. Gootnick, Andrew T (1974). "Locus of control and political participation of college students: A comparison of unidimensional and multidimensional approaches". *Journal of Consulting and Clinical Psychology.* 42 (1): 54–58. doi:10.1037/h0035997. hdl:10150/554618. PMID 4814098.

24. Laverghetta, Antonio. "The Relationship between the Big 5 Personality factors, Locus of Control, and Political Ideology[*permanent dead link*]" Paper presented at the annual meeting of the Oklahoma Research Day, Cameron University, Lawton, OK, Nov 04, 2011. 2014-11-25; URL accessed 14 November 2015
Sweetser, Kaye D. (2014). "Partisan Personality: The Psychological Differences Between Democrats and Republicans, and Independents Somewhere in Between" (PDF). *American Behavioral Scientist.* 58 (9): 1183–1194. doi:10.1177/0002764213506215. S2CID 145674720.

CHAPTER 3

25. Friedman, Z. (2019). 50% Of Millennials Are Moving Back Home With Their Parents After College. *Forbes Magazine*. https://www.forbes.com/sites/zackfriedman/2019/06/06/millennials-move-back-home-college/?sh=f7968cd638ad

26. Moilanen, K., & Manuel, M. (2019, May). Helicopter Parenting and Adjustment Outcomes in Young Adulthood: A consideration of the mediating roles of Mastery and Self-Regulation. *Journal of Child and Family Studies*, *28*, 2145–2158. https://wvutoday.wvu.edu/files/d/382379c3-ed27-45b5-b9cc-eb09619f26cf/helicopter-parenting-study-1.pdf

27. Pells, R. (2017). Middle-class parents damaging their children by not being able to say "no." *The Independent*. https://www.independent.co.uk/news/education/education-news/middle-class-parents-children-not-say-no-spoilt-dr-amanda-gummer-child-psychology-a7886441.html

28. Investigations of college admissions and testing bribery scheme. (n.d.). *United States Attorney's Office District of Massachusetts*. https://www.justice.gov/usao-ma/investigations-college-admissions-and-testing-bribery-scheme

29. Cooper, C. (2015, September 4). *Overly-controlling parents cause their children lifelong psychological damage, says study*. The Independent. https://www.independent.co.uk/life-style/health-and-families/overlycontrolling-parents-cause-their-children-lifelong-psychological-damage-says-study-10485172.html

30. Kim, Y. S. (2016, November 9). Devasted Cornellians "Mourn" Election of Donald Trump at Cry In. *The Cornell Daily Sun*. https://cornellsun.com/2016/11/09/devastated-cornellians-mourn-election-of-donald-trump-at-cry-in/

31. Singman, B. (2016, November 17). Coddling campus crybabies: Students take up toddler therapy after Trump win. *Fox News*. https://www.foxnews.com/us/coddling-campus-crybabies-students-take-up-toddler-therapy-after-trump-win

32. https://www.collinsdictionary.com/dictionary/english/snowflake-generation

33. Twenge, J. M., & Campbell, S. M. (2008). Generational differences in psychological traits and their impact on the workplace. *Journal of Managerial Psychology, 23*(8), 862–877. https://doi.org/10.1108/02683940810904367 Twenge, J., & Campbell, W. (2010). *The narcissism epidemic*. Atria Books.

CHAPTER 4

34. Corr, C. A. (2020). Elisabeth Kübler-Ross and the "Five Stages" Model in a Sampling of Recent American Textbooks. OMEGA- Journal of Death and Dying, 82(2), 294-322. https://doi.org/10.1177/0030222818809766

35. Daigle. (n.d.). The untold truth of Melania Trump. In *MSN*. https://www.msn.com/en-us/news/politics/the-untold-truth-of-melania-trump/ar-BB1iDWb0

36. Addady, M. (2017, May 17). *Mark Cuban predicts 'Huge, huge' losses for U.S. stocks if Trump is elected*. Fortune. https://fortune.com/2016/05/17/mark-cuban-stocks-trump/

37. Borchers, C. (2016, November 7). Donna Brazile is totally not sorry for leaking CNN debate questions to Hillary Clinton. *The Washington Post*. https://www.washingtonpost.com/news/the-fix/wp/2016/11/07/donna-brazile-is-totally-not-sorry-for-leaking-cnn-debate-questions-to-hillary-clinton/

38. Britzky, H. (2017, September 16). 16 things Hillary Clinton blames for her election loss. *Axios*. https://www.axios.com/2017/12/15/16-things-hillary-clinton-blames-for-her-election-loss-1513305545

39. Ryan, J. (2016, November 9). 'This was a whitelash': Van Jones' take on the election results. *CNN Politics*. https://www.cnn.com/2016/11/09/politics/van-jones-results-disappointment-cnntv/index.html

40. John Kasich: President Trump is "in a meltdown." (2020, July 6). *YouTube*. https://www.youtube.com/watch?reload=9&v=Shswrp_hGpk

41. Balz, D., & Costa, R. (2020, February 5). *Romney votes to convict Trump on charge of abuse of power, becoming the lone Republican to breaks ranks* [Video]. The Washington Post. https://www.washingtonpost.com/politics/with-his-vote-to-convict-trump-on-abuse-of-power-romney-will-break-with-his-party--and-awaits-the-consequences/2020/02/05/a76dce74-4841-11ea-ab15-b5df3261b710_story.html

42. Silas, W. (2022, September 18). Action and reaction: Understanding Newton's 3rd Law of Motion. *Probing the Universe*. https://probingphysics.com/third-law-of-motion/

43. Concha, J. (2018, November 6). Bill Maher: 'Bring on the recession' if it means getting rid of Trump. *The Hill*. https://thehill.com/homenews/media/391625-bill-maher-bring-on-the-recession-if-it-means-getting-rid-of-trump/

44. Morton, V. (2023, October 19). Cher vows to leave U.S. if Trump wins in 2024: 'I almost got an ulcer the last time.' *Washington Times*. https://www.washingtontimes.com/news/2023/oct/19/cher-vows-leave-us-if-donald-trump-wins-2024-i-alm/

45. The Constitution of the United States: A transcription. (n.d.). *The National Archives*. https://www.archives.gov/founding-docs/constitution-transcript

CHAPTER 5

46. Kamarck, E. (2020, March 5). *If money can't buy you votes, what can it buy? Lessons from Michael Bloomberg's 2020 run*. Brookings. https://www.brookings.edu/articles/if-money-cant-buy-you-votes-what-can-it-buy-lessons-from-michael-bloombergs-2020-run/

47. Walrath, R. (2011). Kohlberg's Theory of Moral Development. In: Goldstein, S., Naglieri, J.A. (eds) Encyclopedia of Child Behavior and Development. Springer, Boston, MA. https://doi.org/10.1007/978-0-387-79061-9_1595

48. *Kohlberg, Lawrence (1981). Essays on Moral Development, Vol I. I: The Philosophy of Moral Development. San Francisco, CA: Harper & Row. ISBN 0-06-064760-4.*

49. DARAPRIM PRICE HIKE. (n.d.). *McCombs School of Business*. https://ethicsunwrapped.utexas.edu/video/daraprim-price-hike

50. Mitchell, J., & Harlow, B. (2017, September). A review of enhanced interrogation: Inside the minds and motives of the Islamic terrorists who a re trying to destroy America. *Studies in Intelligence*, *61*(3). https://www.cia.gov/static/Review-of-Enhanced-Interrogation.pdf

51. Baker, S. (2018). Michelle Obama said she "stopped even trying to smile" at Trump's inauguration. *Business Insider*. https://www.businessinsider.com/michelle-obama-stopped-trying-to-smile-trump-inauguration-2018-11

52. Michelle Obama: Former US first lady says she has "low-grade depression." (2020, August 5). *BBC*. https://www.bbc.com/news/world-us-canada-53672893

53. Shabad, R. (2020, August 26). Hillary Clinton says Biden should not concede the election "under any circumstances." *NBC NEWS*. https://www.nbcnews.com/politics/2020-election/hillary-clinton-says-biden-should-not-concede-2020-election-under-n1238156

54. https://www.huffpost.com/entry/reince-priebus-trump-deportation_n_58233c0de4b0e80b02ce36ca

55. Dorman, S. (2020, September 19). SCOTUS battle prompts threats, calls for arson: "Burn Congress down." *WDRB*. https://www.wdrb.com/news/national/scotus-battle-prompts-threats-calls-for-arson-burn-congress-down/article_e29b4eb4-fabf-11ea-848b-075bf07761ed.html

56. Ibid.

57. Oppenheim, O. (2023, October 18). Rep. Rashida Tlaib draws fire for not apologizing for saying Israel caused Gaza hospital blast. *ABC News*. https://abcnews.go.com/Politics/tlaib-refuses-apologize-blaming-israel-gaza-hospital-blast/story?id=104085727

58. Helin, K. (2020, July 31). Magic's Jonathan Isaac: kneeling, wearing BLM t-shirt not 'answer' for him. *NBC Sports*. https://www.nbcsports.com/nba/news/magics-jonathan-isaac-kneeling-wearing-blm-t-shirt-not-answer-for-him

59. Schreiner, B., & Lovan, D. (2020, August 24). Kentucky AG in spotlight over Breonna Taylor Probe. *AP*. https://apnews.com/article/virus-outbreak-ky-state-wire-shootings-us-news-d91fa6a9f2d6c8adca5f81b8fd03d55b

60. Connelly, E. (2020, September 26). Women's March co-founder blasts Kentucky AG after Breonna Taylor decision. *New York Post*. https://nypost.com/2020/09/26/womens-march-co-founder-blasts-kentucky-ag-over-breonna-taylor/

61. Hatemi, P., Crabtree, C., & Smith, K. (2019, October). Ideology Justifies Morality: Political Beliefs Predict Moral Foundations. *American Journal of Political Science*, *66*(4), 788–806. https://www.jstor.org/stable/45217042

62. Moore, S. (2019, October 10). Middle-Class Incomes Surging – Thanks to Trump Policies. *The Heritage Foundation*. https://www.heritage.org/markets-and-finance/commentary/middle-class-incomes-surging-thanks-trump-policies

CHAPTER 6

63. Wilkerson, D. (n.d.). *Friedrich Nietzsche (1844—1900)*. Internet Encyclopedia of Philosophy. https://iep.utm.edu/nietzsch/

64. Reuters. (2023, October 3). *See what New York AG said while running for office about charging Trump*. CNN Politics. https://www.cnn.com/videos/politics/2023/10/03/letitia-james-prosecute-trump-2018-comments-running-office-cnntm-vpx.cnn

65. *Are you too male, too pale or too stale?* (Video episode 8374). (2023, November 7). Howie Carr Show. https://howiecarrshow.com/amp/are-you-too-male-too-pale-or-too-stale-tish-james-hate-speech-11-7-23-the-grace-curley-show-hour-2/

66. Peltz, J. (2023, November 29). *Deutsche Bank was keen to land a "whale" of a client in Trump, documents at his fraud trial show*. Yahoo News. https://news.yahoo.com/deutsche-bank-keen-land-whale-180521377.html

67. Steinbeis N, Singer T. Projecting my envy onto you: neurocognitive mechanisms of an offline emotional egocentricity bias. Neuroimage. 2014 Nov 15;102 Pt 2:370-80. doi: 10.1016/j.neuroimage.2014.08.007. Epub 2014 Aug 10. PMID: 25117603.

68. Kilander, G. (2021, June 14). *Obama says Fox News viewers see a 'different reality.'* Independent. https://www.independent.co.uk/news/world/americas/us-politics/fox-news-barack-obama-nyt-b1865842.html

69. Golec de Zavala, A., Dyduch-Hazar, K., & Lantos, D. (2019). Collective narcissism: Political consequences of investing self-worth in the ingroup's image. *Political Psychology, 40*(Suppl 1), 37–74. https://doi.org/10.1111/pops.12569

70. *Golec de Zavala, Agnieszka; Peker, Müjde; Guerra, Rita; Baran, Tomasz (2016-11-01). «Collective Narcissism Predicts Hypersensitivity to In-group Insult and Direct and Indirect Retaliatory Intergroup Hostility». European Journal of Personality. 30 (6): 532–551. doi:10.1002/per.2067. hdl:10071/12977. ISSN 1099-0984. S2CID 54186348. Golec de Zavala, Agnieszka; Cichocka, Aleksandra; Eidelson, Roy; Jayawickreme, Nuwan (2009). «Collective narcissism and its social consequences» (PDF). Journal of Personality and Social Psychology. EBSCO. 97 (6): 1074–1096. doi:10.1037/a0016904. PMID 19968420. Archived from the original (PDF) on 2018-03-24. Retrieved 2022-09-30.* Opposite associations of collective narcissism and in-group satisfaction with intergroup aggression via belief in the hedonistic function of revenge. PLoS ONE 16(4): e0250537. https://doi.org/10.1371/journal.pone.0250537

71. Liberals and conservatives cry "Fake news!" for different reasons. (n.d.). *Nottingham Trent University*. https://www.ntu.ac.uk/about-us/news/news-articles/2018/05/liberals-and-conservatives-cry-fake-news-for-different-reasons

72. Harper, Craig & Baguley, Thom. (2019). "You are Fake News": Ideological (A)symmetries in Perceptions of Media Legitimacy. 10.31234/osf.io/ym6t5.

CHAPTER 7

73. Hart, Paul. (1991). Irving L. Janis' Victims of Groupthink. Political Psychology. 12. 247. 10.2307/3791464.

74. Ssaha. (2019, December 8). *The Salem Witch Trials: A case of mass hysteria.* Real Archeology. https://pages.vassar.edu/realarchaeology/2019/12/08/the-salem-witch-trials-a-case-of-mass-hysteria/

75. Pariser, E. (2011, May 12). *The Filter Bubble: What the Internet is Hiding From You.* Penguin Press. https://www.goodreads.com/book/show/10596103-the-filter-bubble

76. Sarkozy, L. (2017). The media are undeniably biased by their liberal bubble. In *Washington Examiner*. https://www.washingtonexaminer.com/opinion/1230116/the-media-are-undeniably-biased-by-their-liberal-bubble/

77. Usher, N., & Ng, Y. M. M. (2020). Sharing Knowledge and "Microbubbles": Epistemic Communities and Insularity in US Political Journalism. Social Media + Society, 6(2). https://doi.org/10.1177/2056305120926639

78. Gold, H. (2014, May 6). Survey: 7 percent of reporters identify as Republican. *Politico*. https://www.politico.com/blogs/media/2014/05/survey-7-percent-of-reporters-identify-as-republican-188053

79. Morris, K. (2023, December 30). A tiny, shrinking percentage of American journalists are Republicans, study finds. *Fox News*. https://www.foxnews.com/politics/tiny-percentage-american-journalists-republicans-study-finds

80. 2019 El Paso Shooting. (n.d.). *Wikipedia*. https://en.wikipedia.org/wiki/2019_El_Paso_shooting ; 2019 Dayton shooting. (n.d.). In *Wikipedia*. https://en.wikipedia.org/wiki/2019_Dayton_shooting

81. New York Times changes "Trump urges unity vs. racism" headline after backlash. (2019). In *Fox News*. https://www.foxnews.com/transcript/new-york-times-changes-trump-urges-unity-vs-racism-headline-after-backlash

82. Greve, J. (2019, August 6). New York Times changes front-page Trump headline after backlash. *The Guardian*. https://www.theguardian.com/media/2019/aug/06/new-york-times-front-page-headline-changed

83. Reilly, K. (2016, March 8). Donald Trump dismisses Hitler and Nazi salute comparisons. *TIME*. https://time.com/4251138/donald-trump-dismisses-hitler-nazi-salute-comparisons/

84. Sarkozy, L. (2017b, November 20). The media are undeniably biased by their liberal bubble. *Washington Examiner*. https://www.washingtonexaminer.com/opinion/1230116/the-media-are-undeniably-biased-by-their-liberal-bubble/

85. Ehrlich, J. (2018, June 25). Maxine Waters encourages supporters to harass Trump administration officials. *CNN Politics*. https://www.cnn.com/2018/06/25/politics/maxine-waters-trump-officials/index.html Merica, D. (2018, October 10). *Eric Holder on Republicans: 'When they go low, we kick them.'* CNN Politics. https://www.cnn.com/2018/10/10/politics/eric-holder-republicans-when-they-go-low/index.html Cummings, W. (2018, October 9). *Hillary Clinton: You "cannot be civil" with Republicans, Democrats need to be "tougher."* USA Today. https://www.usatoday.com/story/news/politics/onpolitics/2018/10/09/hillary-clinton-cnn-interview/1578636002/ Colton, E. (2021, January 11). *Here are six videos of Democrats calling for violence or physical confrontations that are still active on Twitter*. Washington Examiner. https://www.washingtonexaminer.com/news/1561816/here-are-six-videos-of-democrats-calling-for-violence-or-physical-confrontations-that-are-still-active-on-twitter/

86. Porter, B. (2017, October 6). *OFFICE OF THE COMMONWEALTH'S ATTORNEY - CITY OF ALEXANDRIA*. City of Alexandria. https://web.archive.org/web/20171008071727/https://www.alexandriava.gov/uploadedFiles/commattorney/info/17-001- Simpson Field Shooting-FINAL 10.06.17.pdf

87. Antifa. (n.d.). In *Cambridge Dictionary*. https://dictionary.cambridge.org/dictionary/english/antifa

88. Opinion: Journalist Andy Ngo violently assaulted by Antifa protesters. (2019). In *WSJ*. https://www.wsj.com/video/opinion-journalist-andy-ngo-violently-assaulted-by-antifa-protesters/519A71E1-7C02-44E7-913B-EBC3F3B79560

89. Cohen, R. (2022, February 28). *Family of Capitol rioter said he died of a "broken heart" and blamed the justice system for killing his "zest for life"* [Video]. Business Insider. https://www.businessinsider.com/capitol-rioter-death-family-blames-justice-system-community-2022-2

90. Teargas, pepper spray and batons: Canada police use force to clear Ottawa of trucker protesters. (n.d.). *YouTube*. https://www.youtube.com/watch?v=z56NeiRgCUU

91. Norman, G. (2019, July 1). *Portland mayor should be investigated by feds over Antifa attack on conservative writer, Sen. Cruz says* [Video]. Fox News. https://www.foxnews.com/us/portland-mayor-ted-wheeler-should-be-investigated-by-feds-over-attack-on-conservative-writer-ted-cruz-says Friedman, G. (2019, July 8). Mayor Ted Wheeler, without plan in hand, rejects Portland protest violence. *Portland Oregon Government*. https://www.portlandoregon.gov/omf/article/736698

92. Ngo, A. (n.d.). Portland: Police Chase Down Antifa After They Throw Rocks (20 Sept. 2019). In *YouTube*. https://www.youtube.com/watch?v=OlKFWNSu6Dg

93. Lima, C. (2018, March 1). *'Outrageous' for Oakland mayor to preemptively warn of ICE raid, White House says* [Video]. Politico. https://www.politico.com/story/2018/03/01/oakland-immigration-raid-warning-white-house-response-432147 *ICE to begin immigration raids in US cities on Sunday: report*. (2019, June 21). NBC Bay Area. https://www.nbcbayarea.com/news/local/ice-to-begin-immigration-raids-in-us-cities-starting-sunday-report/155258/

94. Chan, M. (2016, July 7). Minnesota governor doesn't think Philando Castile would have been killed if he were white. *TIME*. https://time.com/4397248/minnesota-gov-mark-dayton-philando-castile-shooting/

95. Furber, M., & Perez-Pena, R. (2016, July 7). After Philando Castile's Killing, Obama Calls Police Shootings 'an American Issue.' *The New York Times*. https://www.nytimes.com/2016/07/08/us/philando-castile-falcon-heights-shooting.html

96. Edelman, H. (2021, September 17). Women caught in viral MAGA hat video sentenced in Delaware Court. *Delaware Online*. https://www.delawareonline.com/story/news/2021/09/17/viral-video-women-caught-who-tore-up-maga-hat-sentenced-delaware-court/8335083002/

97. Gordon, J. (2022, September 23). *Biden is "inflaming his supporters to violence" and "has blood on his hands": GOP tears into President's rhetoric after driver killed Teen "because he believed he was a Republican" - and say if a Democrat was mowed down there would be non-stop coverage* [Video]. The Daily Mail. https://www.dailymail.co.uk/news/article-11242959/Republican-says-Bidens-violent-rhetoric-consequences-North-Dakota-driver-killed-teen.html

CHAPTER 8

98. Vazquez, M., & Carvajal, N. (2020, August 10). *Trump calls on college football games to resume amid coronavirus pandemic*. CNN Politics. https://www.cnn.com/2020/08/10/politics/donald-trump-college-football-coronavirus/index.html Pitofsky, M. (2020, August 28). New Biden ads blame Trump for canceled sports seasons. *The Hill*. https://thehill.com/homenews/campaign/514131-new-biden-ads-blame-trump-for-cancelled-sports-seasons/

99. Lange, J. (2020, June 11). Biden says military would help oust Trump if he loses election but refuses to leave. *SALTWIRE*. https://www.saltwire.com/nova-scotia/news/biden-says-military-would-help-oust-trump-if-he-loses-election-but-refuses-to-leave-460988/

100. Ibid.

101. Einbinder, N. (2019, May 15). Former vice president Joe Biden says he "absolutely agrees" with comment that Trump is an "illegitimate president." *Business Insider*. https://www.businessinsider.com/joe-biden-says-he-agrees-trump-is-illegitimate-president-2019-5

102. D'Souza, D. (n.d.). 2000 Mules. *Rumble*. https://rumble.com/v1238uc-2000-mules-trailer.html

103. *Democrat busted dropping tons of illegal ballots over & over during mayoral election in Connecticut*. (n.d.). [Video]. Rumble. https://rumble.com/v3kwkqy-democrat-busted-dropping-tons-of-illegal-ballots-over-and-over-during-mayor.html

104. *The Tucker Carlson Encounter: Steven Sund*. (2023, August 10). [Video]. Tucker Carlson Network. https://tuckercarlson.com/the-tucker-carlson-encounter-steven-sund/?utm_source=google&utm_medium=paid&gad_source=1&gclid=CjOKCQiAoeGuBhCBARIsAGfKY7wivosGRxkBbwBznDWaGa3-sBqRE9UTTEinKNnpeYmf6sKxLruwE7IaAicbEALw_wcB

105. McCormick, J. (2020, November 13). Bellwether counties nearly wiped out by 2020 election. *The Wall Street Journal*. https://www.wsj.com/articles/bellwether-counties-nearly-wiped-out-by-2020-election-11605272400

106. Tully, S. (2020, November 1). To win, Trump needs 11 million more votes than he got in 2016. *Fortune*. https://fortune.com/2020/11/01/who-will-win-can-trump-win-2020-election-chances-odds-votes-electoral-college-turnout/

107. Kaplan, S. (2017, November 13). Trump raised more dollars from small donations. *Politifact*. https://www.politifact.com/factchecks/2017/nov/13/kayleigh-mcenany/trump-raised-more-dollars-small-donations/

108. Doyle, W. (2021, October 13). *Mark Zuckerberg spent $419M on nonprofits ahead of 2020 election — and got out the DEM vote*. New York Post. https://nypost.com/2021/10/13/mark-zuckerberg-spent-419m-on-nonprofits-ahead-of-2020-election-and-got-out-the-dem-vote/

109. Marcelo, P. (2023, June 12). Claims misrepresent 1,850 boxes of Biden documents at Delaware University. *AP*. https://apnews.com/article/fact-check-biden-trump-delaware-1850-boxes-446929353071

110. Comer, J. (n.d.). The Bidens' influence peddling timeline. *Oversight.house*. https://oversight.house.gov/the-bidens-influence-peddling-timeline/

111. Kurtzleben, D. (2017). Study: News coverage of Trump more negative than for other presidents. In *NPR*. https://www.npr.org/2017/10/02/555092743/study-news-coverage-of-trump-more-negative-than-for-other-presidents

112. Colvin, J. (2015, October 18). Trump's campaign powered in part by small-dollar donors. *PBS*. https://www.pbs.org/newshour/politics/trumps-campaign-powered-part-small-dollar-donors

113. Rahman, K. (2023, July 27). Donald Trump's donors are wildly different from Ron DeSantis'. *Newsweek*. https://www.newsweek.com/donald-trumps-donors-are-wildly-different-ron-desantis-1815734

CHAPTER 9

114. Roper, Cynthia. "political correctness". *Encyclopedia Britannica*, 19 Jan. 2024, https://www.britannica.com/topic/political-correctness.

115. Political correctness. (n.d.). Oxford *Reference*. https://www.oxfordreference.com/display/10.1093/oi/authority.20110803100334599

116. Penley, T. (2023). Pastor facing 10 years in prison for preaching at Canada Trucker blockade protesting vaccine mandates. In *Fox News*. https://www.foxnews.com/media/pastor-facing-10-years-prison-preaching-canada-trucker-blockade-protesting-vaccine-mandates Lewis, M. (2022, October 18). Kari Lake has a point about Jan. 6 rioters being locked up for this long. *Daily Beast*. https://www.thedailybeast.com/kari-lake-has-a-point-about-jan-6-rioters-being-locked-up-for-this-long

117. *Elon Musk* (episode 2054). (2023 October). https://open.spotify.com/episode/7edwvm2c6Ieuzun4xtFYCJ

118. Trahan LH, Stuebing KK, Fletcher JM, Hiscock M. The Flynn effect: a meta-analysis. Psychol Bull. 2014 Sep;140(5):1332-60. doi: 10.1037/a0037173. Epub 2014 Jun 30. PMID: 24979188; PMCID: PMC4152423.

119. Dutton, E., Van Der Linden, D., & Lynn, R. (2016). The negative Flynn Effect: A systematic literature review. *Intelligence*, *59*, 163–169. https://www.sciencedirect.com/science/article/abs/pii/S0160289616300198

120. Pagones, S. (2020). Protests, riots that gripped America in 2020. *Fox News*. https://www.foxnews.com/us/protests-riots-nationwide-america-2020

121. Concha, J. (2020, June 18). Herschel Walker offers sending 'Defund the Police' supporters to lawless countries: 'I want to make them happy. *The Hill*. https://thehill.com/homenews/media/503387-herschel-walker-offers-sending-defund-the-police-supporters-to-lawless/

122. Canova, D. (2020, June 17). *Herschel Walker offers to send people who want to defund police to countries without them*. Fox Sports. https://www.foxnews.com/sports/herschel-walker-defund-the-police-offer

123. Carson, S. (2020, July 31). *He "gave freedom to everyone's voice": A week after shooting death of Bernell Trammell, friends keep his legacy alive*. Milwaukee Journal Sentinel. https://www.jsonline.com/story/news/local/2020/07/31/bernell-trammell-death-milwaukee-shooting-victims-memory-stays-alive/5557683002/

124. Ngo, A. (2021, January 30). *How a Portland radical murdered a Trump supporter — and became a hero for Antifa*. New York Post. https://nypost.com/2021/01/30/how-a-portland-radical-murdered-a-trump-supporter/

125. *VIDEO: Nevada teenager Jonathan Lewis who was severely beaten by gang of youths dies in hospital with his father by his side*. (2023, November 14). Talk TV. https://talk.tv/top-stories/35769/jonathan-lewis-video-nevada-las-vegas

126. Bowden, E. (2020, August 14). Trump says Biden tried to take credit for Israel-UAE peace deal. *New York Post*. https://nypost.com/2020/08/14/trump-says-biden-tried-to-take-credit-for-israel-uae-deal/

127. Carlstrom, B. (2021, May 10). Liberal hypocrisy: How both Obama and Biden have taken credit for Trump's accomplishments. *Amac*. https://amac.us/newsline/society/liberal-hypocrisy-how-both-obama-and-biden-have-taken-credit-for-trumps-accomplishments/

128. Bartiromo, M. (2023, November 10). *Obama has "always" had "a deep hatred of Israel in his heart": Alan Dershowitz*. Fox Business. https://www.foxbusiness.com/video/6340872456112

129. *Transcript: Mayor Adams commits to reducing city's Food-Based emissions by 33 percent by 2030 after releasing new greenhouse gas emissions inventory incorporating emissions from food*. (2023, April 17). [Video]. NYC.gov; City of New York. https://www.nyc.gov/office-of-the-mayor/news/266-23/transcript-mayor-adams-commits-reducing-city-s-food-based-emissions-33-percent-2030-after

130. Ohanian, L. (2012). Why shoplifting is now de facto legal in California. In *Hoover Institution*. https://www.hoover.org/research/why-shoplifting-now-de-facto-legal-california

131. Wallace, A. (2022, April 7). *The shipping container backlogs at east cost ports are now bigger than those on the West coast*. Business Insider. https://www.businessinsider.com/supply-chain-shipping-containers-east-coast-backlog-west-coast-2022-4?op=1

132. AP. (2024). Biden won't face charges after retaining classified documents from days as VP, senator. In *CBC News*. https://www.cbc.ca/news/world/biden-classified-documents-doj-reportm 1.7109403#:~:text=Hur's%20report%20said%20many%20of,were%20retained%20by%20%22mistake.%22

133. Comer, J. (2023, September 13). Comer: Oversight Committee has uncovered mounting evidence tying Joe Biden to family business schemes. *Oversight House*. https://oversight.house.gov/release/comer-oversight-committee-has-uncovered-mounting-evidence-tying-joe-biden-to-family-business-schemes/

CHAPTER 10

134. Hains, T. (2023, August 15). Newt Gingrich: This is the greatest constitutional crisis since the 1850s. *RealClear Politics*. https://www.realclearpolitics.com/video/2023/08/15/newt_gingrich_indictment_is_a_desperate_effort_by_corrupt_machine_to_destroy_their_most_dangerous_opponent.html

135. Hanson, V. D. (2023, August 15). Commentary: Joe Biden's race against the truth. In *The Tennessee Star*. https://tennesseestar.com/commentary/commentary-joe-bidens-race-against-the-truth/admin/2023/08/15/

136. Campanile, C. (2017, January 11). Schumer predicted intelligence officials would 'get back at' Trump. *New York Post*. https://nypost.com/2017/01/11/schumer-predicted-intelligence-officials-would-get-back-at-trump/

137. *Trump attorney speaks out on the Mar-a-Lago raid*. (2022, August 10). [Video]. Fox News. https://www.foxnews.com/video/6310711257112

138. Pefley, A. (2022, August 26). *Unredacted portions of FBI affidavit raise questions, expert says* [Video]. CBC Austin. https://cbsaustin.com/news/nation-world/unredacted-portions-of-fbi-affidavit-raise-questions-expert-says-mar-a-lago-raid-former-president-donald-trump-former-fbi-agent-stuart-kaplan-classified-documents

139. Hanson, V. D. (2023, August 3). Two sets of laws for two Americas. *The Blade of Perseus*. https://victorhanson.com/?s=Two+sets+of+laws+for+two+Americas

140. *Opinion: Joe Biden forced Ukraine to fire prosecutor for aid money*. (2019, September 23). WSJ. https://www.wsj.com/video/opinion-joe-biden-forced-ukraine-to-fire-prosecutor-for-aid-money/C1C51BB8-3988-4070-869F-CAD3CA0E81D8

141. Herlihy, B. (2023, December 21). *Special counsel in Trump case unconstitutional, former Reagan AG says*. Fox News. https://www.foxnews.com/politics/special-counsel-trump-case-unconstitutional-former-reagan-ag-says

142. *Why Stacey Abrams owes Georgia an apology*. (n.d.). WSJ Podcasts. https://www.wsj.com/podcasts/opinion-potomac-watch/why-stacey-abrams-owes-georgia-an-apology/091051ab-adcf-436e-93c9-33d67041d9f0

143. Itkowitz, C. (2019, September 27). Hillary Clinton says Trump 'knows he's an illegitimate president' as she backs impeachment inquiry. In *Independent*. https://www.independent.co.uk/news/world/americas/us-politics/hillary-clinton-trump-impeachment-illegitimate-president-2016-election-cbs-a9122986.html.

144. McArdle, M. (2020, October 9). Hillary Clinton maintains 2016 election 'Was not on the level': 'We still don't know what really happened.' *Yahoo News*. https://news.yahoo.com/hillary-clinton-maintains-2016-election-160716779.html?guccounter=1&guce_referrer=aHR0cHM6Ly93d3cuZ29vZ2xlLmNvbS8&guce_referrer_sig=AQAAAClVrZTsw2WinhOUBtWob3TRkuBSDRklMIagvCwiOFyZnhqRt0Azt8AOXv8D5hg3o5XVlkLn_YErnRl6-Igiajfd nlWBozogLdAjiqGYBrdGBmElO4Pr44UFfOkRAPRxTFCYQRCKq3DpOVtuRF9hU2502ZNEFqQ904hjj7eZ02-y

145. Barraby, T. (2020, December 31). *Barbara Boxer claims "no comparison" between her 2004 electoral college objection and Hawley's*. Fox News. https://www.foxnews.com/politics/barbara-boxer-no-comparison-2004-electoral-college-objection-hawleys

146. Hanson, V. D. (2023, August 3). Two sets of laws for two Americas. *The Blade of Perseus*. https://victorhanson.com/?s=Two+sets+of+laws+for+two+Americas

147. Hall, A. (n.d.). Biden campaign released guide of how to respond to "crazy MAGA nonsense" from relatives during the holidays. *Fox News*. Retrieved November 23, 2023, from https://www.foxnews.com/media/biden-campaign-released-guide-respond-crazy-maga-nonsense-relatives-holidays

148. Stanton, A. (2023, November 20). Democrat Calling for Trump to Be "Eliminated" Sparks MAGA Fury. *Newsweek*. https://www.newsweek.com/dan-goldman-calling-trump-eliminated-sparks-maga-fury-1845364

149. Hayes, G. (2023, December 13). Univision journalist defends Trump interview that caused liberal firestorm: We offered "fair platform." *Fox News*. https://www.foxnews.com/media/univision-journalist-defends-trump-interview-caused-liberal-firestorm-we-offered-fair-platform

Made in the USA
Las Vegas, NV
18 July 2024

92582577R00095